Heads Up!

Heads Up!

Practical Sports Psychology
for Riders, Their Trainers,
and Their Families

JANET SASSON EDGETTE, Psy. D.

DOUBLEDAY
New York   London   Toronto   Sydney   Auckland

PUBLISHED BY DOUBLEDAY
a division of Bantam Doubleday Dell Publishing Group, Inc.
1540 Broadway, New York, New York 10036

DOUBLEDAY and the portrayal of an anchor with
a dolphin are trademarks of Doubleday, a division of
Bantam Doubleday Dell Publishing Group, Inc.

Book Design by Beverley Vawter Gallegos

In order to ensure their privacy, I have changed the names
and identifying characteristics of my clients.

Library of Congress Cataloging-in-Publication Data
Edgette, Janet Sasson.
Heads up!: practical sports psychology for riders, their
trainers, and their families / Janet Sasson Edgette.—1st ed.
p.   cm.
Includes index.
1. Horsemanship—Psychological aspects.   I. Title.
SF309.E3   1996   96-14457
798.2′01—dc20   CIP

ISBN 0-385-48017-2
Copyright © 1996 by Janet Sasson Edgette
All Rights Reserved
Printed in the United States of America
October 1996
First Edition
1   3   5   7   9   10   8   6   4   2

Dedicated to

my husband, John,
without whom this—and
so much else—would never
have happened.

છે

And in loving memory to
Allyn Schechter
and Wayne Carroll.

Acknowledgments

I'd like to thank Joel E. Fishman, my agent, for his assistance and support for the book. Thanks also to Frances Jones, my editor at the Doubleday Equestrian Library. Many thanks are in order to Mandy Lorraine, editor at Practical Horseman, for her enthusiasm and profound insightfulness. I'd also like to thank my trainer, Peter Vanderkallen, and Louise Serio, for their valuable input to the chapters for professionals. And special thanks to my sister, Carol, for all her loving support and, finally, Nancy Peterson, my very first riding instructor, way back when at Camp Forest Acres.

You don't dance to get to the other side of the floor.

—Philosopher Alan Watts

Whether you think you can, or think you can't, you're probably right.

—Henry Ford

Contents

Part One: For the Rider . . .

Part Two: For Trainers and Instructors

Part Three: For Everyone

Part One
For the Rider . . .

Preface

A WOMAN in her late forties arrives for her first appointment. She tells me about the anxiety she feels before horse shows, an anxiety so overwhelming that it seems to strip her talent away each and every time she enters the arena. She's a dressage rider and says that at show times her body freezes up the way ice crystallizes on a shrub. She becomes immobilized, breathless, mentally blank. Sensing her nervousness, her horse stiffens. She worries that he feels betrayed by her. When she comes out of the arena, "Anne" has no memory of her test, only the awareness that the bad thing has happened again. She wonders all the way home why she can't "just relax."

Anne and I take our time during the first session. I ask her to walk me through her anxiety attack, to bring me inside her head so that I too can feel her sense of derailment, her panic, her disappointment, her disgust. She does this, and I learn about her characteristic style of *generating* anxiety, of *experiencing* anxiety, and of *overcoming* anxiety. I find out where she's good at managing anxiety and, more useful still, where she is able to pre-empt it altogether. I help her discover and create mental tools that enable her to disengage from her anxiety so that she can accomplish what she wants to *despite* it. I help her find ways to distract herself from it, to ignore it, even to befriend it. As Herman Munster and his son Eddie understood, a dragon isn't nearly so scary when it shares your home and eats your dinner scraps.

We do some hypnosis, too. Anne learns to become mentally absorbed both on and off the horse and to find the quiet places in her mind. She lets images of marionettes and arthropods, with their articulated joints, effect the kinds of changes in her body that no verbal self-command ever could elicit—independence of movement, elasticity, lightness, elongation in her spine. As Anne describes how the letters in the competition arena cause her to choke, I teach her to make them sing out to her instead. "A" for atta girl! . . . "B" for breathe nice and easy . . . "C" for cool and collected . . .

Anne was one of my earliest sport psychology clients, and I will never forget my joy in witnessing the rediscovery of her aptitude and adoration for her sport. I've gone on to assist hundreds of riders to regain a lost sense of confidence; learn to create one for the first time; overcome the trauma of a bad fall; develop a bolder or more decisive attitude; correct undesirable riding habits, such as leaning forward, carrying one's hands too high, or looking down; modify their self-image so that it is consistent with changes they've made; feel better prepared mentally for competition; feel less vulnerable to the anxiety-provoking presence of an old trainer at a show; develop a sharper focus of attention; manage the physical discomfort that may interfere with their riding; clarify goals; dispel the worries that have been negatively affecting their riding; and resolve tensions between them and their trainers or family members. These clients include competitive and recreational riders both, and range from Pony Club to Olympic levels.

For quite some time now, psychology has been growing in popularity as a tool for improvement in all sporting endeavors. Elite athletes have become more candid about their reliance on sport psychologists, and even amateurs have started to recognize that their smaller scope of athletic involvement also warrants the benefits of working with such professionals.

Unfortunately, many people have come to think of psychology as either dry and impractical or pedantic and presumptuous—understandably so, given its portrayal in the media and how it has often been conducted in practice! The field is evolving, though. The processes of change in individuals are better understood, and there is greater emphasis on creating active, collegial, and collaborative relationships between professional and client. There is also now an emphasis on the capacity for rapid transformation. I, and others like me, encourage people to see themselves as resourceful, resilient, and adaptive. Play, humor, searching conversations, rituals, and inspiration are taking their rightful places in the consultation room. This movement has been afoot in the fields of clinical and counseling psychology for years now, and I've begun extending it into the realm of sport psychology, especially for the equestrian.

I have designed this book specifically to help the equestrian athlete enhance his or her experience of riding, training, competing, and otherwise doing business with horses. The rider's need for mental improvement may be performance-oriented, as in the case of someone looking to allay show nerves, get rid of a bad riding habit, perform more consistently under pressure, develop more confidence in jumping on muddy tracks or going fast during timed jump-offs, and the like. It may also have less to do with performance or outcome (winning in the show ring) than with the rider's level of enjoyment or comfort with the sport, as in conquering vague fears of going fast on horseback or of riding alone, lapses in general confidence, loss of trust in one's own judgment or that of a trainer's.

But there is another thrust to this book, one that takes it beyond much of the other material available to athletes, and certainly to equestrian athletes. That is its coverage of the many different relationship issues involved in sport. An increasing number of questions raised by private clients and seminar attendees alike have to do with ways in which they may better manage the interpersonal and familial stresses that arise from their riding commitment. This book specifically addresses such matters as riders wanting to balance their passion for riding with their devotion to a spouse or family; parents wanting to know how to evaluate training schedules for their young children; incorporating sportsmanship into training programs geared so tightly toward winning championship points; and similar concerns. Other matters within the domain of the sport psychologist but largely ignored in the equestrian literature are also dealt with in this book. They include the psychology of teaching and of running a riding business, relationships between trainers and the parents of the minors they have in training, and the masked signs of stress often experienced by trainers, riders, and members of the riders' families.

Too many people think of sport psychology as offering a limited (and old) fund of knowledge dealing only with performance-related matters. *Heads Up!* is my contribution to changing this view. I also offer readers specific insights, ideas, and practical strategies that can enhance their entire riding experience. Essentially, this book is what I talk about with clients, and what questions they ask me. Also, it is what I discuss with family and friends and what I am learning myself. I've been riding for over thirty years now, first showing in the junior hunter, jumper, and equitation divisions at shows up and down the East Coast in the early 1970s, and currently showing in the schooling and amateur owner jumper divisions. I live this stuff, and I wrestle with these questions of managing anxiety, creating positive mental sets, and balancing home life, family, career, and riding. I hope you will find the book as pleasurable, interesting, and useful to read as I did in writing it.

JSE

Chapter One

The Magic in Sport Psychology

EVERYONE THINKS that he or she knows what sport psychology is: a little bit about breathing the right way, something about positive thinking, and a lot about relaxing. And since people figure that they've been breathing fine for years, and, for the most part, think in a pretty upbeat fashion, and can generally relax on lots of occasions, they conclude *Why bother learning something I already know?* Furthermore, these people figure that they already know the point is to be able to do all this while you ride, and that if they could be doing it, they *would* be doing it. If they can't, then a sport psychologist's telling them to do it isn't going to be of much use anyway.

But these aren't the only things sport psychology is about. Yes, deep and easy breathing, a relaxed and supple body carriage, and a positive mental set are desirable—especially in riding. But sport psychology can offer far more than this. Equestrian sport psychology, in particular, can create for riders of all disciplines and levels numerous opportunities to change the old habits and attitudes they have toward riding that compromise performance or the enjoyment of the sport. It offers riders a variety of ways to enhance their feelings of confidence, competence, or self-control. It can also help riders learn to tap effortlessly into that intuitive, right-brain, automatic way of riding that characterizes our best rides.

There's more, too. Sport psychology can teach individuals about preparing mentally for lessons, for competitions, or for their own training regimens—not canned routines, but ones that are tailored to each rider, individualized routines that both inspire and affirm. And then there are the ways in which sport psychology can help the "too-intense" rider temper his or her seriousness and learn to play in sport, to enjoy the process of riding rather than being committed exclusively to winning. In addition, there will always be riders trying to overcome the trauma of a bad fall, or put behind them what turned out to be a disastrous school, or get over the death of a beloved horse or pony. The relationship of client and professional comes under the heading of equestrian sport psychology, as does the rider's relationship with his or her family, and the family's (usually parents') relationship with the trainer.

Consider the following situations presented to me in my practice (names, identifying information, and some noncritical details have been changed to protect confidentiality in these and all other examples throughout the book):

- an amateur hunter rider trying too hard to be perfect finds that her methods keep making matters worse;

- a trainer's preoccupation with winning at shows interferes with her enjoyment of riding;

- a young girl who took a bad spill off her pony loses her confidence in him;

- an adult rider returning to the sport after a ten-year hiatus finds himself physically and mentally challenged;

- parents of a thirteen-year-old girl are concerned that she has become too competitive with her friends and barn mates;

- a Grand Prix jumper rider loses her heart for showing after her favorite and best horse dies;

- a teenager has trouble getting attached to his new horse after the old one is sold;

- a single mother who learned to ride as an adult loves the sport but worries about becoming disabled from a fall and having no one to care for her two kids;

- members of a family stretched to the max financially begin to show the stress by arguing with one another;

- a young man has trouble controlling his temper while riding;

- an eight-year-old junior rider has crying spells before and after every horse show.

People often wonder exactly who it is that comes for sport psychology services and what it is that client and professional do together. I see normal people who wrestle with the kinds of stressors that are particular to this sport or common to all kinds of competitive endeavors. Some of us are handed (or inadvertently create) more stress than others; some of us deal with these stressors better than others, some worse. Most of those who come face situations that are not crazy, not unusual, not insurmountable. They simply need some psychological tools for getting back on track, where they have been operating fine for months or years, or a reminder about the tools and other personal resources they already used in the past that they can call on to overcome similar situations. Nobody is alone with these problems although people often feel that way. They wonder if anyone else has ever faced the things they do, and are relieved to find out that their experiences and worries are shared silently by innumerable others. Sport psychology becomes more humanized as soon as you humanize the problems people ask for help with.

You **Can** *Change*

People have long underestimated the flexibility—the wonderful elasticity—of the mind. Thought, memory, feeling, attitude, perspective, self-concept, and outlook can be modified constructively in any number of ways. And they can be modified within a brief period of time and through relatively simple means. The rest of this book shows you how to do the modifying, at home and on your own.

Helping people change psychologically used to be thought of as a long-term endeavor. It was believed that you needed to "uncover" memories and feelings from your past (namely, bad ones), that you needed then to talk about them for months or even years with a dispassionate therapist, and that you (largely) needed to experience the process as distressing. The discipline of psychology has changed dramatically in the past several years, and the changes are positively reflected in the treatment for helping people feel and do things differently. Psychologists and their clients now recognize that change processes can be uplifting and inspiring and even fun. In the following pages I'll bring this new technology of change into the realm of equestrian sport psychology.

What does the new technology look like? Well, it's a focus on action and change-making and discovering little things that can make a big difference. It's a focus on the present and future rather than the past, and on finding solutions rather than analyzing problems. That single mom who's worried about getting hurt learns to speak to her trainer about setting parameters of risk that she can be comfortable with. And the teenager with the new horse decides to visit his old horse's grave and ask "permission" for the new partnership, thus freeing himself from the past. The man with the temper resurrects his childhood use of heroic role models to contain his tempestuous behavior in favor of a more sympathetic approach to handling horses.

Another feature of this technology of change is its emphasis on utilizing a person's existing resources instead of assuming that he or she is without mental and personal skills, tools, or expertise. Thus, the adult returning to the sport after a long time reminds himself of how he successfully overcame the unfamiliar mental challenges of a new job following a career change several years earlier. And that amateur hunter rider who, years ago, learned to give up trying to be the "perfect" parent discovers how to stop being the "perfect" hunter rider and simply enjoy her sport; ironically, that buys her eight good fences. And how about the family that was arguing about money? Well, they recall how they were able to overcome other family stress periods and rally together as a group, such as when Grandpa suffered a stroke and needed to move in, and when Mom had to travel out of town regularly for a six-month period and the household hung together by a thread.

In addition to the sport psychology clinics I do, I devote a considerable amount of my practice to teaching general psychotherapy skills to a variety of mental health professionals. In these seminars, I emphasize ways to make the change process efficient, relevant, psychologically meaningful, and appealing. I'll emphasize these same things for you throughout the book, as you will be taking on for yourself, in part, the role of sport consultant or psychologist. You'll use this book to become your own "change agent," to discover for yourself in the privacy of your home or barn the many ways in which you can make a difference in your riding, or in how you feel about your riding, or in the relationships affected by your riding.

OK, Now, What's This About Magic?

In 1992, the skater Paul Wylie won an Olympic silver medal in Men's Figure Skating in Albertville, France. He had been considered a dark horse, having been plagued for years with the problem of freezing up at big competitions. What went on in his mind right before his Olympic winning performance? A quote from *Henry V* remembered by Wylie as follows: "We're not in the enemy's hands. We're in God's hand." In an article describing his experiences in Albertville, Wylie explained that he had imagined King Henry addressing his troops, seeing him as Shakespeare's version of Rocky.

This majestic little jewel of literature was all that was needed to inspire Wylie and draw from him a magnificent performance. Wylie didn't have to do anything but think of that quote. He didn't have to rehearse it or memorize it or say it a prescribed number of times to himself before the event. *"I kept hearing . . ."* is how Wylie described it—a gentle and passive process out of which came a mental set that liberated nearly unbeatable skating. That a thought or image can effect so powerful a response in someone in so effortless a fashion is magic to me.

Here's more magic. Several years ago an American track and field star and high jumper named Pat Matzdorf won a national championship. Everyone crowded around him after the event, asking what he had done differently that year to perform so well. Did he eat better? Sleep more? Use special shoes? No, none of those things, Matzdorf replied. It was just that he hadn't shaved that morning, and it had made him feel "mean"! That was his explanation, soup to nuts. So simple. So easy. Contrast this natural, self-resourceful sport psychology with the type of intensive mental skills training you more commonly hear and read about and then ask yourself which *you'd* rather be doing.

Sport psychology never had to be as effortful, technical, and forced as it's become for so many of its practitioners and their clients. The process of change can be made simple and pleasurable, especially if we heed the lessons provided by the natural wisdom of our bodies and minds. We can learn a lot from the Wylies and Matzdorfs and other athletes who have found innate inspiration to excellent performance. But there is another way, too, by which sport psychology can be made into a living and dynamic process, and that is through the process of *resource retrieval.*

Retrieving Personal Resources: Using What's Already There

As mentioned earlier, resource retrieving refers to the discovery of one's personal strengths in the form of latent abilities, attitudes, memories, mental skills, and the like. These latent (or hidden or forgotten) strengths are revived and made accessible to the sport psychology client as part of an expanded repertoire of mental skills.

Let's use the example of a rider who has lost confidence in her ability to get her horse through a cross-country course. We'll assume that once, not so long ago she was very confident on course but has since lost that feeling. Maybe she lost it because of a fall, or because of a few bad schooling experiences or because of a gradual erosion of confidence. The important thing to know is that she *was* confident. She does not, therefore, have to "start from scratch" in order to become confident once again. She has a history of confidence when riding cross country, and memories of that experience are stored in her brain. This rider needs help in reconnecting to that feeling, in finding her way back to it. And that is much easier than facing the task of building confidence from the ground up.

Now let's make the situation a little more challenging by choosing someone who has no memory of confidence in jumping cross-country fences. Even that rider doesn't have to start from scratch, because there's likely to be another area in her life where she does feel confident and from which she can "borrow." Imagine that she is in the business of land development, for example; she scouts out properties that could turn into good commercial or residential sales. So this woman, despite her liability on a cross-country course, does in fact already have a familiarity and even a skill base in *dealing with new terrains and overcoming obstacles.* The key here is helping the rider to recognize and transfer that ability—that resource—into her riding experiences.

Just because a talent lies outside the domain of riding doesn't mean it can't be used when you're on horseback. Think back to the man who parlayed his career mental skills into better riding mental skills. Or the woman who transferred her learning about "imperfect parenting" into an approach we could call "imperfect (but effective) riding." These interventions are founded on recognizing the importance of "neutral" mental skills in sport performance. Decisiveness, judgment, communication skills, perspective-taking, patience, and responsiveness to nonverbal cues are all mental skills that serve us in living contexts that span work, love, play, and sport; they are rudimentary tools in place, already. This recognition is a far cry from the sport psychology or general therapy client seeking assistance and feeling that he or she has little to offer by way of solutions or other psychological capital.

This business of resource retrieval works in a variety of situations presented to equestrian sport psychologists. A dressage rider who wants to develop a sharper focus of attention when entering the arena doesn't need to start from square one. He already knows how to attend sharply; he does it every time he watches a movie, every time he examines a wound on his horse's leg, every time he becomes absorbed in that first bite of holiday cake. All this rider has to do is look into his own history and find how he consistently focuses during those other occasions. Once he taps into that ability, he can begin to teach himself to do it elsewhere—for instance, during his warm-up, or as soon as he hears the warning bell, or the moment he enters the arena at A. Some riders have found it helpful just to know that they have inside themselves the very abilities they're looking for, and then look forward to reconnecting to it, even though they may not yet have figured out exactly how to do so.

The following are some examples of riders using the concept of resource retrieval to "unstick" themselves from a particular riding snag:

✔ One adult recreational stock seat rider, who had given herself the gift of riding for quitting her daily wine habit, developed a fear of cantering after her horse ran off with her. Although she logically believed cantering her horse to be safe, the mere idea of it would evoke enough anxiety to cause her to hyperventilate. I asked this woman how she ever gave up drinking. She replied, "I made up my mind—that was it." And that *fortitude,* so useful in overcoming one difficult problem, became the resource around which our work together was spun.

✔ A male saddle seat rider, who authoritatively and very successfully ran his own business, had a habit of letting his horse get away with murder, both on the ground and while being ridden. He'd let the horse nip, squirm while being groomed, quicken his paces, and look around inattentively during lessons. He was distressed by his seeming inability to control his mount. But all he had to do was figure out what allowed him so comfortably to *"be the boss"* in the workplace, and enact that with his equine partner. For this man, the bugaboo had been a life-long compassion for animals that prevented him from setting limits on their behavior, no matter how appropriate, necessary, or humane.

✔ A hunt seat pony equitation rider who was having trouble establishing a sense of partnership with a leased pony was able to use *her experience of working satisfactorily with a classmate of whom she was not so fond* on a joint school project. She transferred her learnings of compromise, negotiation, and tolerance to the building of a working relationship with the new pony.

✔ A jumper rider training a green horse was having trouble relinquishing control over every aspect of their approach to fences, and her horse was not being given opportunities to figure things out for himself. Reminding this rider of the *process she must have had to go through letting her teenage son psychologically separate from her* and figure things out for himself helped her to do likewise with her new young charge.

In all these cases, the client and I found a solution to the current problem by figuring out how he or she had dealt with situations that seemed different on the surface but that actually had something in common. Most people aren't aware of the psychological tools or resources they have available to them, while others are aware that they have a lot of "life experience" but aren't sure how best to take advantage of that wealth of wisdom. Milton H. Erickson, a great psychiatrist and hypnotherapist who practiced in Phoenix, Arizona, until his death in 1980, said it best to his clients: "You know more than you think you know."

How to Use This Book

The chapters that follow will teach specific sport psychology strategies that have proved useful to riders from all different disciplines. Many of these techniques follow the lines discussed in this chapter, where simple, small alterations in how you think or talk about something result in enduring changes in your riding in effortless, almost magical ways. Other strategies are more technical in nature, and resemble the traditional vehicles used by sport psychologists to help athletes reach their goals. Think of the material as a smorgasbord of sorts, where you can look over the different offerings and choose for your own plate the ones that appeal to you and that work best for you. A little trial and error is always in order with this kind of thing. Sample some things, go back for seconds, try something new. The goal is to assemble a collection of mental tools that can help you more easily, quickly, and effectively meet your riding goals.

And then there are the chapters that don't deal so much with specific mental strategies as they do with specific issues of equestrian (and often other) sports. These are as much a part of the mentally prepared rider's repertoire as are the latest sport psychology techniques, and an understanding of them can frequently do more to alleviate a riding problem or catapult a rider into the winner's circle than any mental rehearsal or visualization could ever do. *Bon appetit.*

Chapter Two

Breaking Myths
About Relaxation

I DIDN'T REALIZE it at the time, but my first lesson in the paradox of relaxation came when I was ten years old. I had been invited to Kathy Reece's house for a sleep-over and was very excited at the prospect. She had acres of land in back of her house and a Shetland pony in the garage-cum-barn. Going to Kathy's house was cool.

My only problem was that I suffered from homesickness, and my track record for sleep-overs was lousy. I hadn't yet made it through the night without my mom's being called to come get me. All the pronouncements by friends' mothers that I was going to "have so much fun that I'd never want to leave" were to no avail. The more they promised, the earlier in the evening the pangs of homesickness began.

But Kathy's mother seemed to know instinctively something the others didn't, so when my mother and I arrived at her house with my little flowered suitcase, she *didn't* promise us that I wouldn't get homesick. She gently ushered me through the front door, turned to my mom, smiled, and said, "Well, Mrs. Sasson, I guess you'll probably be hearing from us around ten or so! See ya later!" And from that moment on I never got homesick again.

Whether or not Mrs. Reece had thought much about what she was saying, her intervention was brilliant. She was the first person to expressly give me *permission* to get homesick! And when I realized this many years later, I discovered how much more powerful it can be to surrender to what we can't control than to battle it again and again and again.

Our Delusions of Control . . .

Many of us move through life trying to exert or maintain control over its many different parts. We want to feel that we have control over what we feel, do, and think—and that's just for starters. We also want to feel that we have control over the safety of our loved ones, the predictability of the future, the course of our day-to-day activities. Some of this we do have, but not as much as we'd like to believe. We delude ourselves at times, thinking that we're "in control" of some event, but then we get humbled—or, worse yet, shocked—by tragedy into the awareness that we can control only some things, not all. We cannot control all the dimensions of our own experiences all the time, and the biggest, truest witnesses to this are the numerous and largely counterproductive battles of athletes to relax on command.

Classical, physiological relaxation, with its slowed heartbeat, diminished pulse rate, muscular slackening, and dampened swallow reflex, is not a simple, voluntary response of the human body. Winking at someone is, as is hopping on one foot. So too doing a crest release or a half halt. But relaxing is not. Taking a deep breath *is* under our voluntary control, and can be used by some athletes to achieve a more relaxed frame of mind or body state. But taking a deep breath is not the same as relaxing. If it were, none of us would ever *not* be relaxed again; we'd all just go about our business breathing deeply all the time.

Real relaxing comes *after* you feel right about what you are doing or about what's happening. That is, it's almost always secondary to, or a direct outgrowth of, the right mental set. Now, that mental set will be different for different people. For some, it is a sense of being *composed,* while for others, *confident, aggressive, grounded, focused, powerful,* or *contained* better describe their best head set. Some feel their best, and are most relaxed, when they find themselves with a *devil-may-care* attitude. Basically, people are liberated from their anxieties and are as relaxed as is possible, given the situation, once they feel ready to do what it is they have ahead of them. There's no relaxation technique like preparation, and even that's no guarantee.

All this doesn't even take into play the fact that for some athletes—and this includes riders—relaxation is the last thing they are looking for! Look at Picabo Street, 1994 Winter Olympics American silver medalist in Women's Downhill Skiing. Her "method" seems to be getting to the starting gate within minutes of her start time—and she still has yet to get her skis, gloves, and goggles on! Now, this is exactly the kind of situation that would turn me into jelly. I'd more likely than not make arrangements to sleep on the mountain the night before, just to be sure I got to the event on time the following day. Street's style is definitely not relaxed, but it works for her.

And then there's Tommy Moe, the American gold medalist skier in Men's Downhill (and silver in Men's Super G) at these same 1994 Games who did his runs a few days earlier. He's up there before his run, yawning! On camera, no less. Now that's what I call relaxed.

The Mental and Physical Characteristics of Ideal Performance States

When Lars-Eric Unestähl, a Swedish sport psychologist, did some research on the peak performance states of elite athletes, he discovered some interesting things about the way these athletes experienced their minds and physical bodies. These competitors characterized their performance states by the phenomena listed below. Not every one had all of them, but by and large these were the predominant, repeated mental and physical experiences of the elite track and field athletes included in Unestähl's study.

1. **Amnesia** for their performance, or a global and diffuse recollection of the event, devoid of the specific details of their decisions, adjustments, or actions;

2. **Intense concentration** to the point of dissociating, or **"disconnecting,"** from the surrounding environment and all its distracting stimuli;

3. **Detachment from sensations of pain,** so they weren't feeling physical pain, even though *an awareness* of the body being uncomfortable or in pain might be present;

4. **Perceptual changes,** such as tunnel vision, time distortions, enlargement of objects, and altered sensations in the body;

5. **An increased sense of power and control.**

Note that there is *no* mention on this list of being relaxed. It is not the end-all and be-all of good athletic performance. It's not necessarily a bad thing, but don't worry if you're not getting it. There are other, better experiences to be striving for that can serve to distract you from too much emphasis on feeling relaxed, and give you a better sports advantage, to boot.

Moreover, few people actually ever get to function in that idealized relaxed state. I don't care what others say about "once you get to a certain level, you don't get nervous." Jim Kelly, the Buffalo Bills quarterback, admits to throwing up in the locker room before every game. I've spoken to enough upper-level equestrians from a variety of disciplines to realize that nervousness comes with competitive sport, and while a few don't seem to experience anxiety in any recognizable way, most of them do to some extent and have learned to accept it as part of the challenge of riding. The question for competing equestrians is not whether they can do a passage or a clean obstacle course or a flawless equitation work off, but whether they can do it on demand, consistently, and at the competition with lots and lots of people watching. The key is riding well *despite* one's anxiety, and most pros (and I mean that to include pros in the literal sense as well as the amateurs who approach their sport with a professional attitude) know this. Listen to what Andre Agassi, tennis champ, has to say about this: "When you step onto a court, it's like another person takes over. The nerves are so intense, and all of a sudden there's a sense of peace. It's incredible."

You see, sport professionals like Agassi and Kelly don't worry too much about finding ways to exorcise anxiety or nervousness. They prefer to spend their mental energies on aspects of their game over which they have greater control and that will make a bigger difference. Do likewise.

Different Strokes . . .

I was recently talking about these things at a seminar when a question arose. A man in the audience said, "I've liked some of the relaxation techniques that I've learned. And sometimes taking a few deep breaths right before I go into the ring helps me settle down. Can't this be a useful aid for some riders?" You bet it can.

But another rider walks into my office and spills onto the coffee table half a dozen books on relaxation techniques. "I've read them all," she sighs. "The more I read and the harder I try, the less relaxed I get and the more like a bozo I feel. Isn't there another way?" You bet there is.

Just as people are different from one another in their senses of humor, work ethics, and relationship styles, they are different in their styles of coping with anxiety. One person's anxiety may not even look like any other's. Some riders freeze up into a paralyzed state, become unable to talk or think clearly, and get so absorbed in their anxiety that they won't hear the ring announcer calling their name. Yet others are all over the place, so to speak, their uncontainable anxiety running amok. They talk a mile a minute to anyone in sight, and orient to every sound and movement within a one-mile radius of where they are standing. You can only figure that if two people can be that different in how they manifest their nervousness, they are going to be different in how they manage it. It's the lack of tailoring to the individual athlete's personality style that accounts for a lot of failed sport psychology efforts.

Are You a Group A or a Group B Rider?

In the chapters to follow, I'll teach you a variety of anxiety management and performance enhancement strategies from which you can choose. I have found that riders generally fall into two camps in terms of anxiety style, each camp doing better with certain strategies and techniques than with others. Refer to the chart on page 21 for a general breakdown. You'll see, too, that some work well for both—it just depends on the personal preference rather than anxiety style. But don't get locked into the selections under your group. Try what appeals to you and experiment; you have nothing to lose.

Two (Very Different) Approaches
to Anxiety Management

Are You Type "A"?
If So, Then Consider . . .

- Traditional relaxation techniques
- Deep-breathing techniques
- Self-hypnosis
- Yoga or meditation
- Music on a Walkman
- Any activity that absorbs your attention and distracts you (i.e., hand-held electronic games)

Are You Type "B"?
If So, Then Consider . . .

- Chunk it down . . . Start small!!!
- *Study* it as a fascinating physiological response
- *Learn to anticipate* the anxiety, so it never catches you by surprise
- *Channel* your nervous energy into constructive pursuits
- *Reinterpret* the meaning of your anxiety . . . Define it as an opportunity to practice managing being anxious
- *Prescribe* to yourself the problematic situation
- *Interrupt* your pattern of nervous behavior . . . Do the same thing if you need to, but just do it differently!
- Clear yourself out and come back later

And for Both Types . . .

- Mental rehearsal
- Mind-body response training
- Hypnosis and self-hypnosis
- Rituals and symbols
- Riding resource rooms
- Worry buddies
- Worry creatures

Group A: The "I Like to Have Something Concrete and Specific to Do When I'm Anxious" Rider

A sizable number of riders, but probably not the majority, will do better with specific strategies that they can use to actively deal with their nerves. They like feeling that they have concrete tools, something they can apply to the problem at hand. They like having something they can do. Riders like these do very well with relaxation techniques (such as progressive muscle relaxation, where you alternately tense and then relax different muscle groups throughout the body), breathing routines (such as diaphragmatic breathing, where you breathe in your nose on the count of one and exhale slowly through your mouth on the count of two . . . three . . . four, making sure to breathe from your lower abdomen and not high up in your chest area), and other like strategies (don't forget about things like meditation, yoga, or simply listening to good music on a set of headphones while tacking up or in the privacy of the cab in your truck). These riders get a lot of mileage out of these techniques, both in terms of their riding performance and their riding experience. You may, too.

Group B: The "Less Is More" Rider

The other kind of rider doesn't have as much luck with these techniques. The harder these guys try to relax, the worse things get. Attention to the problem in any fashion always seems to make the problem grow larger. At best, they remain as anxious as when they started out; often they feel worse.

I've discovered that, for these riders, other approaches work better, approaches that help them go with the flow of events, in a dynamic rather than a static orientation toward the internal experience of the moment. They learn to go forward through their experience, be it of physical nervousness, mental anxiety, or a repetitive worry. Since stopping to fix it doesn't work, finding a way to go with and accept the experience becomes a more viable answer. And paradoxically, this laying down of arms against the undesirable event or feeling sows the seeds for its quiet disappearance. In its place come brief moments of relaxation or composure. I think of these as moments of grace, as little jewels of feeling all right, that disappear as quickly as you notice their arrival. But they come back again, another moment here or there, like a horse flexing for the first time—he drops his head, relaxes his jaw, oops, there it goes, OK, you wait for it to come back and it does and, oh, it's delicious. If you try to grab at it and make it stay . . . well, you know what happens. It's the same with this relaxation response.

Let me tell you a funny story about "chasing" relaxation. A non-equestrian client of mine was taking a few sessions to help her deal with her phobia of intrusive medical procedures (intravenous tubes, injections, blood drawings, and the like). Unfortunately, she was involved in medical treatment that required her to receive regular and frequent injections at home.

Lorie had learned a relaxation technique from another therapist that essentially required her conscious effort to get relaxed. She would use the technique, and when she was done, she'd turn to her husband (who was standing there with a syringe) and cheerfully say, "I'm ready"! Immediately afterward, knowing the injection was coming, she would then absolutely lose it, going right back into a panic, and halting the whole process. This would go on and on, to no avail. That's when she decided to call me to see if there was another way.

Lorie and I had a good laugh during her recounting of this scene, but I could appreciate how unhumorous it had been for her. The poor woman was chasing her relaxation response all over the darn room, and it remained as *there* as ever.

And of course it would. Lorie and her husband never had a chance. Since Lorie needed the injection sooner than she was going to be cured of her needle phobia, I thought it better to help her cope with the anxiety she was going to experience rather than try for a home run and somehow make it disappear. This was the tactic we chose and, along with some hypnosis and some talk about changing her perspective on such issues as control, we were able to have Lorie handling her shots and IVs and other pokes and prods nearly like an old pro. Just remember, there are no command performances when it comes to getting yourself to relax.

There Is Another Way . . .

Chunk It Down

When trying to get more relaxed while riding, think small. This is truly one of those times in life where less becomes more. One moment of feeling relaxed is an entirely sufficient starting point. Later, it can expand into a few moments, strung together, and then into an even longer stretch of time, when you not only are aware of feeling relaxed and comfortable but can maintain the feeling even after you become aware of it—no simple feat! Many people lose the very experience they've tried so hard to get once they become aware that they have it. It's normal and a very common experience.

Think about it this way. When we work with our horses, encouraging them to become lighter, softer, more relaxed, we are usually delighted to feel it happening and don't do anything to "make it stay." We know better, and recognize that if you command the softness and suppleness to stay, you'll break the integrity of the process and lose the whole thing. So we're content in the beginning with a little bit of response, for instance, when a horse is first learning to relax under tack or with the added demands of more sophisticated movements. Eventually, we ask for and get a little bit more, or get it for a little bit longer period, and so on. So why should we be more demanding toward our own relaxation response than we are with the horse's? It's as elusive for either species, but somehow we believe that our bigger brains should enable us to override that. Well, we're pretty silly. Look instead for the smaller, sweet moment and let it expand into something larger in its own way.

Another way to chunk things down is to select those few moments when it is most critical for you to feel relaxed, rather than seeking a time-unlimited goal. For instance, would it be good enough, at least for starters, if you were able to achieve some relaxation for the moment or two before you enter the show ring, instead of trying to get it for the entire half hour before, what with tacking up and schooling and what not? Similarly, what about just feeling good on the drive to the barn for your lesson, rather than being nervous for that twenty-minute period *and* the hour that you tack up and get ready? Maybe you'll be nervous when you get there, maybe you won't, but at least that one piece of your riding experience—the drive over to the barn—can feel different. This happened to one rider client of mine who was surprised at how much of a difference it made to her when she was once again able to enjoy the drive from her suburban home to the barn. She still got nervous while riding, but at least she had back her triweekly country drive. Remember that a little bit of relief goes a long way to help you feel that change is possible, and that a long-standing pattern of anxiety is beginning to fray at the edges. A change in a pattern of behavior or internal experience is always a good sign that something is different, that something is happening.

Another idea is to work toward getting some state of muscular comfort or relaxation in just one or two parts of your body rather than everywhere. Let it be enough; and again, gradually build from there. For example, many riders do better focusing on relaxing the wrists instead of the arms, the neck instead of the upper body, the ankle instead of the lower leg.

Take the Fight Out of It

The best slogan by far when dealing with "unrelaxed" feelings is *"Demilitarize! Demilitarize!"* Taking the fight out of trying to get relaxed should be the first step toward altering your state of mind. Locking horns with anxiety only makes it a larger monster. Empowered by all the attention you've given, it puffs up its chest and roars even more loudly. Here is what you can do instead:

A. Study Your Anxiety as a Fascinating Physiological Response

Believe it or not, some people are able to approach their anxiety response—whether it be tremors, butterflies, a dry mouth, or generalized body tension—as a peculiar but interesting physiological response to a particular situation. I used this strategy to help an overweight man eat less by having him relate to his hunger pangs *not* as a cue to eat but, rather, as a fascinating physiological response of his body to a certain need state. A middle school science teacher, he was able to enjoy this little twist on what had become for him a clear trigger to eat. So you, a rider, can examine your anxiety response as if you were an academic doing research, or a graduate student completing a thesis. "Study," for example, how quickly breath rate can change in the fifty feet between the warm-up area and the in-gate. "Analyze" the difference in frequency of negative thoughts between when you're trotting and when you're cantering. Get so far "into" the anxious response that you come out the other side, where it begins to feel different to you, the way a familiar word looked at too long starts to look foreign, unrecognizable.

B. Anticipate the Anxiety

Anticipating the thing that leaves you feeling as if you've been jumped in a blind alley often works to take away its power. Where there's no surprise, you can't get thrown. Much of this strategy is based on the concept of changing your relationship with your anxiety, that is, interacting with it in a different way. It may not make it go away, but it can alter drastically how it affects you, which is almost as good.

How does one anticipate anxiety? By getting curious about it: when is it going to appear? The night before? The morning of some special occasion? Right before an important ride? Begin a dialogue with the part of your personality that gets anxious and ask it when it thinks it's going to make it's debut and if it has in mind something special today or just its old ordinary way. Play with the part of you that gets anxious, befriend it, let it know that it doesn't have the power to catch you off guard anymore. Whimsy is tension's greatest annihilator.

C. Channel the Nervous Energy into Constructive Pursuits

Taking the energy that comes out of being anxious and turning it into something useful is an age-old technique to transform nervous tension. At the very least, if it makes you feel no better, you'll have something to show for it. This is exactly what I do every time I spend the night before a horse show bleaching my white saddle pads and cleaning the rubber treads of my stirrup pads with a toothbrush. If I didn't get a little high strung before shows, my tack wouldn't look half as good as it does.

D. *Reinterpret the Meaning of Your Anxiety*

All this refers to is changing the definition you give to how you feel. So, instead of dreading an impending sense of nervousness, define it as an opportunity to practice managing anxiety states—batting practice, if you will, for future or even more anxiety-provoking conditions. The more times you have to practice, the better you'll become at managing it successfully. Plain and simple.

One professional baseball pitcher used to suffer from pregame anxiety attacks that left his heart pounding so badly he didn't think he could play. When he learned to "reinterpret" this response as his body's signal to him that he was "on" and ready to roll, he began to stop reacting negatively to his performance jitters. A jumper rider I worked with was able to reinterpret the nervous, burning-stomach sensation she'd get at the bigger shows as her cue that she was hot and ready for blast-off!

E. *"Prescribe" to Yourself the Problematic Situation*

In the spirit of Mrs. Reece's intervention, try giving yourself express permission to have whatever degree of anxiety you "need" to have on a particular day. Known in the mental health field as "prescribing the symptom," this therapeutic technique works well when trying hard to make something not happen usually just makes it worse. Insomnia, uncontrollable blushing, obsessional thinking, and, of course, anxiety, are good examples of these kinds of conditions.

Because these symptoms are typically experienced as involuntary— one feels little or no control over their appearance and disappearance—it hardly makes sense in the first place to try to "not have them happen." Yet most people who battle such things do just that, primarily because they are sick and tired of them and don't really know what else to do.

Well, there's something else to do: Tell yourself that you not only

will have some anxiety the next day for your horse show or lesson or
trail ride, but that you *must* have some—at least, say, twenty or thirty
minutes of it. You tell yourself that you'll spread it out over the course
of the ride or over the course of the whole day, but that you must have
at least twenty or thirty minutes (whatever length selected) of real,
full-fledged anxiety, no ifs, ands, or buts. If your problem is a run of
the same two or three negative thoughts that intrude on you just
before going into the show ring or arena, then prescribe to yourself
the task of having no less than four or five such thoughts come at you
this time.

Sound crazy? I can imagine. But let me tell you what usually happens. The anxiety or the intrusive thought never quite materializes.
Charged with having to manufacture such thoughts consciously, most
people find themselves unable to do so, at least for any significant
length of time. It's a lot like trying not to think of a white elephant,
even once, for the next half hour (an impossible task—try it and see)
versus telling yourself that you must think nonstop of a white elephant
for the next half hour (an equally impossible task). Prohibitions of
thought always tempt more than the prescription. This simple but
seldom acknowledged gem of psychology, when pressed into service
in sport, can be shaped into a valuable tool for the athlete contending
with performance nerves and similar mental phenomena.

What else can happen when you prescribe your symptom to yourself? Well, let's say you do manage to make the anxiety come for
twenty minutes, or are able to make four or five rather than two or
three negative thoughts greet you at the in-gate. What good is this?
Suddenly, you feel an odd (but welcome) sense of control over the
symptom. *Gee,* you think, *it "listened" to me. I made it come when I wanted
it to. Maybe I can make it go when I want it to.* If you can increase the
frequency or intensity of a symptom, why wouldn't you begin to feel
that you can decrease it as well. Sometimes, just that thought of "possibility" is enough to change how you feel about your anxiety
episodes.

And yet another thing sometimes happens with symptom prescription: playing this way with your problems offers a whole new
perspective on what seemed an impossible, intractable problem. The
craziness and whimsy of it all—inviting the very difficulty that you

have for months, even years, been trying to escape from—can alone break up what might have been becoming a frustrating approach to the management of your anxiety. For those who appreciate Eastern ways of thinking and approaching life, this strategy is much like Taoist teachings of blending with, rather than countering, life forces in your attempts to master them.

F. Find a Personal Symbol

Using a personal symbol or metaphor for anxiety management (mind or body) is another option for riders. For example, can you liken yourself to a tuning fork, you know, one of those metal instruments that sound a specific pitch when struck? Why am I telling you to think of yourself as a tuning fork? Because it is a great symbol of something that radiates tension (albeit mechanical in this instance). This action is the very opposite of what most people do when dealing with tension. They concentrate hard on "making it go away," whereas a more useful thought is to let it pass over or through, and then away. Many riding clients of mine have been able to use this idea of a tuning fork as a personal metaphor for letting tension move through and out of them. Read the chapter on Ritual and Symbol for more about this and for other examples.

G. Interrupt the Symptom Pattern

If someone wanted to stop biting her nails but hadn't yet been able to get rid of the urge, I might suggest that she go ahead and bite them for the time being as long as she does so in the reverse direction of how she usually proceeds. This way, the nail biter doesn't have to wait until she is able to fully control her habit before discovering a way to change it. Changing a habit, or a symptom like anxiety or intrusive thinking, is a promising precursor to ending it; it breaks the integrity of what had seemed automatic, involuntary, or otherwise unavoidable. So, if you find your worst bout of anxiety occurs while you're tacking up, see if you can have it occur instead as you collect your tack from the tackroom. If it usually comes to you in the form of hyperventilation, see if you can have it come instead as stomach butterflies. If you can't stop those two or three negative thoughts from coming at you at just the wrong time, can you at least have them say something different?

H. Switch Tacks and Clear Yourself Out

If you feel tense while waiting for the hunt or horse show or trail ride to begin, and you and your horse start to argue about how much time is too much time to respond to a half halt, don't keep pursuing the half-halt business. Walk a circle, do a lopey canter in two point, ask for three or four steps of a shoulder-in—just do something else for a little while. If you are about to enter the show ring or dressage arena, those last few moments of perfecting a movement—if you're feeling desperate and tense—won't go half the distance of simply walking around, regaining your mental composure, and bowing out of the impending fight with your horse.

I. Put Your Attention and Energy Elsewhere

Essentially, the idea is to forget about trying to rid yourself of your anxiety. This is not glib advice; it's a viable strategy. You accept that you are going to be anxious, and that it is the price of doing business. It comes with the territory. It's recognizing that there rarely is sport without personal challenge, and there rarely is challenge without anxiety. So give up on the improbable, and turn your attention toward something you can control, or control more easily, such as practicing your two point or your canter departs or your figure eights. *"I still get anxious but I don't care anymore!"* is the response I hear from clients who've been able to do this. It's lovely.

J. Consider Your Anxiety in a Broad Context

Let's face it. For those of us who do get anxious about doing well, the riding ring or show ring is hardly the only place where we do so. We like to do well, and often want others to see us as doing well. It happens to us in the workplace, on the tennis court, during a game of Pictionary. Winning, or presenting oneself as accomplished, is often part of our personality, like it or not.

So what about considering your performance-related anxieties (as opposed to those springing from fear, or from real dangers connected with your riding) not as a "riding" problem but as part of what you, as an individual, bring with you to the sport and must learn to deal with constructively? If you know yourself to be a perfectionist and this has hindered your getting some work assignments done on time, you don't speak of having a "work" problem but of being a little too, well, perfectionist for your own good. You try to tone it down some. Do the same with your riding. Think of the constructive management of your performance anxiety as one more dimension of a broader landscape of riding challenges, like developing a deeper seat, a better eye for a distance, a softer hand.

And, Finally, *Remember* That

• *It's Important Not to Get Stuck Waiting for Perfection*

Whether it's your physical and technical readiness to perform, or your internal sense of well-being, don't wait until it's perfect. You'll never feel ready that way. *"Going on what you got"* is a slogan I encourage in riders with performance anxiety; it can help them adopt more of a process orientation than a strictly outcome one.

• *You Are Not Alone!*

Almost everybody gets nervous, and most struggle with it one way or another—some just a little bit, others more so. Look around at your next horse show or clinic and practice saying to yourself that there is (despite no one's ever saying it) a shared, communal experience going on under all those hunt caps, derbies, and Stetsons.

This chapter on relaxing and managing anxiety states really fits to a T the metaphor of a smorgasbord described in the first chapter. Some of the items presented will appeal very much to some people, a little bit to others, and only mildly to some. Certain readers will have scoffed at an idea that another scoops right up. So be it. Everyone gets nervous and gets comfortable in his or her own way, and the only way to figure out your best means of shedding an uncomfortable mental or physical state is to try something else. Be bold, and experiment with strategies that are far from your customary way of handling things. Then try something closer to home. Eventually, you'll be able to put together a collection of things that you can do or think or reflect on that will change your experience of feeling nervous and render the whole matter of trying to relax an issue of the past. Let it go the way of the dinosaurs: extinction.

But anxiety is not the only thing riders have to think about in their efforts to ride better or ride more enjoyably. The chapters that follow in this section describe techniques for altering different aspects of your riding experience. They include some of the more familiar ones, like mental rehearsal, and some that aren't so familiar, like the riding resource room, or perhaps hypnosis. In each chapter are criteria to help you determine whether or not the technique or strategy is good for you. Mix and match, and remember, the goal is to put together a sport psychology program for yourself that fits your own needs and personality. Read through them all, even the ones you may be tempted to skip because they're "not you." And then see where "you" are at by the book's end.

Chapter Three

Ideomotor Training

(Or, Watch What You Think and Say, and
Whatever You Do, Don't Say Don't!)

- *A woman stands at the entrance to a dressage arena and, in her mind, listens to the final movement of Beethoven's Ninth. The grandeur of the music playing inside her head has the effect of creating in her body a matching carriage of grandeur. When it's time, she marches right into the ring.*

- *A hunt seat equitation rider practicing on the flat without stirrups feels himself becoming stiffer and stiffer until he feels like the Tin Man in* The Wizard of Oz. *He plucks from his mental shelf the image of a marionette, with its loosy-goosy limbs and independence of movement. It works to unlock him like a can of WD-40. Instantly, his body is transformed.*

- *A hunter rider comes down to the final line of fences at a horse show—fences 7 and 8—the ones where for whatever reason he always finds himself looking down. Using his ideomotor training skills, he thinks of the soda 7-Up!, which reminds him to lift his eyes as he comes to fence number 7. He smiles the whole way down the line at his private little joke.*

Taking Advantage of the Mind-Body Connection

The highway between mind and body is open and runs both ways. Our often fruitless attempts to separate these dimensions of experience are contrived merely for convenience and simplification. Our bodies continually organize themselves around whatever active thoughts and ideas and images are circulating through the conscious and subconscious parts of our minds, a process that goes on with or without our awareness. That's why it's so important for you to get the right images, the right self-talk, and the right pictures in your mind's eye in order for things to go the way you want them to.

What Is Ideomotor Training?

Serious athletes know that in order to improve performance beyond a particular point you must discipline the mind as well as the body. This is a neglected axiom in a lot of training programs. Interestingly, the reverse holds true, too: advanced chess players are known to train by running and swimming because of their awareness that without a certain degree of physical fitness they would never be able to sustain the levels of mental concentration needed for tournaments.

Ideomotor training (it is also called mind-body response training) means teaching yourself to use certain mental ideas as a trigger for a specific behavioral responses. The term reflects this connection between ideas *(ideo* is from the Greek for "thought") and *motor* (from the Latin for "movement"). An ideomotor response would be a rider's thinking of the word "loose" and her body, seemingly on its own, becoming loose. Some people liken it to a process of mental programming; this is a little too techno sounding for me, but it can serve as a working model for others.

I use the term ideomotor training broadly in my sport psychology work to include a person's capacity to also evoke certain feelings and attitudes by an idea. The feelings and attitudes are then reflected in the rider's behavior while she is riding. For instance, she thinks "attack," develops feelings of decisiveness and aggressiveness, and then attacks the jumper course in front of her with a decisive, aggressive ride.

Ideomotor training is based on the psychological principle of ideomotor functioning, the body's capacity to manifest whatever is on or in the person's mind. You'll recognize ideomotor functioning when I remind you of how a mother, thinking *open your mouth* while trying to get her baby to eat, unwittingly opens her own mouth. Or think about being in the passenger seat with a new driver and feeling your own foot move as you think the driver should be stepping on the brake. These actions are not characterized by conscious forethought but by a subconscious process. So the woman standing by the arena thinks of the grandeur of that symphony, and her body opens up, becoming grand. The equestrian rider thinks of his marionette and finds his shoulders, his elbows, his lower back unlocking. The hunter rider sees his soda can, looks up, and finds his fences. It's a graceful, almost invisible transformation.

Applied to sport psychology, ideomotor training becomes a simple technique to help you, the rider, redesign the image and dialogue in your head in order to establish a regular, subconscious association between the image or words and a desired physical response.

The great thing about this technique is that it works for you *while you're riding*. It doesn't require that you set aside time before to rehearse or prepare yourself. Rather, it's a way to "reset" your attitudinal or physical state in the midst of your ride if you find yourself needing a little self-correction. But while ideomotor responding can become an instantaneous phenomenon once it is learned, it does require some practice to get it set. The key is to make a solid association between whatever idea, in the form of thoughts, images, or words you call up from your "mental tool box," and the desired physical state or feeling. Since associations between any two things grow stronger over time and with repeated connecting, your practice of thinking the thought, image, or word and of generating the desired feeling will help stamp in this response. Once it is established, it will sustain itself automatically simply by your repeated use; you won't need to practice it once it's working for you. However, if you don't find yourself using it, the technique's effectiveness can fade. Then you'll need to give yourself a "booster shot" with a practice session or two.

Who Should Use Ideomotor Training?

- Those who wrestle with negative thoughts, words, or images as they ride, or at critical points in their riding—for instance, when they approach a jump, when they are standing at the in-gate at a show, or on the mounting block.

- Those who have negative self-talk that they haven't been able to change.

- Those who phrase their self-instruction in negative terms; for example, "Don't look down," or "Don't grab at his mouth!"

- Those who want to quickly change what they're doing on their horse in terms of their application of aids, their posture, their mental attitude.

The Two Most Common Mental Errors Riders Make and How to Use Ideomotor Training Instead

When people go about instructing or correcting themselves as they ride, they usually do one (or both) of two unhelpful things. The first is using negative terms, such as "Don't look down" or "Don't stiffen up." The second is relying too much on left-hemisphere processing, which results in very logical, rational language-based directives. Neither is very effective in sports. Let's look at each one so that you can really see the pitfalls and revamp how to set yourself up mentally and physically for your best riding.

A. Don't Say Don't!

When my firstborn was an infant I considered his naptimes to be a gift from the heavens. I could shower, eat undisturbed, make a phone call, go to the bathroom by myself. Anyone's waking him up prematurely was punishable by . . . well, by horrible things. "He who awakens, does the caretakin's," became the working motto.

Now, the upstairs bathroom was right next to Casey's room, so whenever I went in I'd remind myself to be very quiet, especially when sliding back and forth the mirrored cabinet panels. I would stand in front of the cabinet telling myself, *Do not rattle the cabinet, don't, whatever you do, **rattle that cabinet!*** And then I'd watch myself, without fail, move the one mirrored panel over to the other side with shaking hands, clattering hairspray against mousse, tumbling makeup into the sink, and, of course, rattling the panels against each other the whole way back and forth. I did lots of unexpected caretakin's until I learned about programming my movements, and about the influence of self-communication and mental images on motor actions.

How many times have you walked into the ring for your ride or lesson, silently proclaiming, *I'm not going to stiffen up on my horse today!* If you are like most riders, you'd be surprised to find out that's exactly what happened. That was because you inadvertently "programmed" yourself for the *stiff* ride. You see, our brains don't have mental representation for the words *don't* and *won't*. These words are abstractions, with no concrete mental symbol. So what happens is that over and over in your mind only the idea of stiffening up is circulating—the *don't* or *not* part has been lost. *"Stiffen up"* is weaving in and out of your cerebral lobes all throughout your warm-up. And your arms and legs say, *Oh, I get it, you want "stiffen." No problem!* Dammit, you say, I can't believe I got stiff today—that's just what I *didn't* want to happen!

It's for this reason that people who tell themselves *Don't stop breathing,* wind up breathless after their go, why people who tell themselves *not to lean at the jumps* end up with mouthfuls of mane, and why people who tell themselves *not to drop their eyes (or hands)* end up staring at the ground or clutching wither. These people should be telling themselves what it is they *want* to do or have happen, in succinct and simple terms. How to do this? Two steps:

- Begin by defining your ride. What is it that you're looking for more of when you ride? What is it that you have the most trouble maintaining? What is it that leaves you when you find yourself in trouble while riding? Is it a *feeling of softness,* a *sense of composure,* a *mental set of confidence?* Maybe it's *independence of body movement,* or a *sense of groundedness,* or *mental organization,* or *focus,* or *trust in your eye for a distance,* or *patience,* or a *deep seat.* Maybe when you get nervous you forget to keep your shoulders open, sink your heels down, carry your hands, or keep your horse going forward. Once you have defined the feel or movement or position or attitude, then you can compose the phrase or word that perfectly matches it. The idea here is to keep it short, tight, and positive. One or two words will do. Examples:

— the phrase *"eyes up," "7-Up"* for keeping you looking up.

— the words *"shoulders open," "open sesame," "straight up!"* for keeping your upper body correct.

— *"lots of patience to combinations"* for keeping you sitting chilly as you come down to that triple.

— *"sink," "be a lead fishing weight," "stretchy legs"* for helping you develop a deep-seat feeling.

— *"cool as a cuke"* for keeping your show nerves quieted.

One client of mine was a hunter rider who used the word *elegant* as her cue for a soft, buttery ride; she'd silently say this to herself as she made her courtesy circle and found it very helpful. In fact, the message she left on my answering machine following her participation in the National Horse Show, for which we were preparing her, was that the tools she'd learned "made a world of difference . . . it was the best I ever walked into the 'indoors.' " My husband, John, would use the word *chilly* to achieve a patient attitude and counteract his tendency to do too much whenever he had a long approach to a fence.

• Change any negative phrases that you've been using into positive ones. Remember that negative words such as *don't, not,* or *never* don't register in your mind and in your subconscious, so you'll end up with the very idea you don't want swimming around in your head. Therefore, instead of saying or thinking to yourself *I will not snatch at my horse's mouth if he gets jiggy,* convert the phrase to *Still hands.* Instead of promising yourself that you will *never look down to check diagonals again,* think of *feel your diagonal. Don't forget not to drop your eyes around the turn* becomes *Turn your eyes up,* with that little play on the word *turn* for added effect. *Don't ride backward to the water jump* becomes *Be a motorboat!* And *Don't get tense passing the cow pastures on the trail* converts to *pastoral scene* or even *boring bovines.*

B. Translating Left-Hemisphere Thinking into Right-Hemisphere Language

The other problem that people get into when self-instructing is relying too much on left-hemisphere processing, characterized strongly by its love of logic, rationality, and analysis, at moments or in situations when we are not good at responding to logic or being particularly rational. After all, most of our self-talk occurs when we're nervous or excited. While the previous section helped you select better words for improving your ride, this one will help you select better pictures, or symbols, and use them to change what you do on top of your horse.

Look at some examples of how people's emotions and behavior can be positively influenced by means other than a lot of back-and-forth, distracting—or, worse yet, self-critical—inner dialogue:

- A person gazes at the seashell on his desk and is reminded of his recent summer vacation at the shore; he finds himself smiling.

- A woman watches a commercial for nail polish and without thinking pulls her fingers from her mouth.

- Someone else hears a favorite Russian symphony come over the airways and rises to the majesty of the sound with regal posture.

Now, nobody told that first man to feel good. Nobody told the second woman to stop biting her nails. Nobody bugged the third guy to fix his posture. Each thing happened as a natural response to a symbolic representation of a pleasurable or desirable state—in these instances, a relaxed vacation, pretty nails, grandeur. This is more representative of right-hemisphere processing, where we interpret and respond to the world around us, or the world within us, primarily through shape, sound, metaphor, and symbol. The right hemisphere is that part of our brain which responds to music instead of written words, that recognizes faces instead of names, that interprets emotions, gives a mental voice to passions, and understands how colors can represent feelings. We can often effect changes in our emotional and physical state by brief contact with these images, sounds, or even smells. The changes work better for our sport purposes because they can happen in a less consciously engineered way than by directing oneself with language-based instruction or a straight directive. Think about it. Would that first man's smile and moment of serenity have come so naturally or felt so authentic had his coworker come by and said, "Hey, you look spent! C'mon, cheer up—think about that vacation you just came back from!" And how would that other guy have responded if he unexpectedly caught himself in the hallway mirror looking slouched? Maybe he'd have straightened up for a moment, maybe not. But it would have felt more "by the stick" than the carrot, a generally inferior and certainly less inspiring means to an end.

Here's another point. Listening to yourself go through a litany of verbal instruction takes a lot of time. Galloping five strides out from a fence is not a lot of time. Crossing the diagonal of a dressage arena is not a lot of time. Waiting in the start box is not a lot of time. Better to just go with a picture of a melting stick of butter to get your upper body to relax than to say, over and over, *Now don't go getting all tense, after all it's only a horse show.*

Here's how to capitalize on the differences between how the two halves of our brain function and start translating left-hemisphere directives into right-brain inspirations:

- Again, begin by defining the ride that you want. Are you looking for soft? Balanced? Aggressive? Flip any negative phrases (i.e., not tense, not too racy) into their positive counterphrases (relaxed, slow, or quiet). Now the trick is to find an image or symbol that represents these counterphrases, something that you can condition yourself to respond positively to while riding. You can even think of the counterphrases or words as your *antidotes*, concise visual expressions that counteract the pinpointed problems.

    For example, you can't consciously make yourself relax on horseback, but you can usually allow yourself to relax if you bring to mind an image of softness. Why not picture a melting stick of butter, a soft rag doll, or a warm shower stream following you above your head wherever you ride? The image can become your body's cue for generating the desired response.

But don't expect your body to respond fully right away. Be satisfied with just a little response at first: your shoulders let down a bit, your neck relaxes a bit, maybe you feel a change in a few back muscles. Let that be enough until you find yourself able to respond more richly, within a shorter period of time. Eventually you'll find yourself responding in flashes of a second. Initially, during the practice stages, you'll refer to the image repeatedly and practice "letting" your body soften a little bit here or there, and then gradually expand the response throughout your body. Practice this first when you are off your horse, and then, when you begin to feel yourself responding pretty regularly, try it mounted.

Here's another example of using an antidotal mental symbol. Suppose you think that you'd ride better if you had a greater independence of movement in your body parts. You'd like, for instance, to be able to apply more leg without your arms and hands tensing, or you'd like to be able to do softer half halts without your back stiffening. But trying consciously to relax your back while using your hand aids has not done the trick. Instead, you learn to think of marionettes whenever you wish to change how your body feels at the moment— beautiful, hand-crafted marionettes whose every joint can be tweaked into operation independently of the others. And now, you find that over time you can use this symbol to immediately and effortlessly effect a response of independent movement among your own body parts, either by conjuring up the image of a marionette or by simply saying to yourself, *"Be Pinocchio!"*

Do you have trouble applying your aids firmly enough for your horse to take you seriously? Teach your body to respond more assertively when your horse misbehaves by choosing an "I'm the boss" symbol—a judge's gavel, for instance. Or, as one of my clients selected, a seafaring captain's hat. Don't limit yourself only to visual symbols, though. One client of mine, a clarinetist trying to recoup feelings of boldness on cross-country courses, found that humming the first few bars of "Fanfare for the Common Man" did the trick for her! Another discovered an ability to respond quickly and effortlessly with calm by imagining the color indigo blue.

In a sense, these symbols work like bridges between our left and right hemispheres. They marry the intellectual, analytic wisdom of our left brain with the holistic, symbolic nature of our right brain, resulting in a synergism of abilities. We could not ride if we relied on one type of hemispheric functioning alone. And, as many of us discover, we don't mesh the two sides very well when we try to force things.

One other valuable feature of these symbols is that they can function as "reset buttons" for riders who find themselves floundering mentally or physically while riding. When called on, they can get you back on track instantly by bypassing your conscious attempts to right yourself and allowing it to happen more effortlessly. Like those tiny red buttons seen on a host of mechanical appliances, they can be pushed once when nothing's working and—presto!—the garbage disposal or whatever starts functioning beautifully again.

Ideomotor Response Training and Affirmations: (Very) Distant Cousins

It's important to remember that ideomotor training is not the same as saying affirmations to yourself. Affirmations involve saying or thinking positive statements about your riding capabilities or about how you feel inside at the time. It is used not so much to transform how you feel or how your body is feeling as it is to buttress your confidence or motivation level. I generally avoid using this strategy, because I find it too artificial.

People use affirmations in an attempt to superimpose a feeling or attitude on top of what they are really feeling in the hope of covering over anxiety or fear or lack of confidence, or pushing it away by emphasizing something more positive. I have found that affirmations never feel true to the heart; they often leave the person saying them with a brittle sense of confidence. My clients seem to do much better when respecting how they do actually feel, and dealing more honestly with that in their attempts to feel different. To me, there's something disrespectful about affirmations, especially when they don't reflect how you feel at that moment, whether or not the statement is objectively true by external standards or judgments (i.e., "I'm ready to do this next level of cross country course"). There are always stylistic differences among professionals as well as among clients; I say that if you have been using affirmations with good results, then by all means continue, but my preferred way of handling things with athletes is more along the lines of the adage "To thine own self be true."

Summary of Ideomotor Response Basics

- Remember that whatever it is your mind is picturing or thinking, your body will try to do. It thinks that's what you want.

- Negative phrases and negative images aren't useful. Picture or say or think what you want to do, not what you are trying to avoid doing.

- Use the technique both to establish overall quality in your riding and to handle specific problems.

- Repetition is important. Practice summoning up your catchword or slogan or your symbolic antidotes. Figure out which negative thoughts bombard you the most so that you can have better ones at the ready.

- This is a sport psychology technique that does require some practice. You must spend a little time establishing the connection between the positive phrase, word, sound, or image and the mental or physical response desired so that when you are riding the response will come to you effortlessly and automatically. Remember (especially those of you who encountered Psych 101 in college), you are essentially building up a conditioned response to a stimulus. What will happen with practice is that the response will come more and more quickly after you call up your word or symbol; it will become stronger and more powerfully felt; and, finally, it will come to you in a variety of settings, including the more stressful ones. Therefore, you may first find it working only when you're at home or while riding by yourself, where you're hardly nervous, then later on in lessons, and eventually in shows or during more challenging rides.

• And, finally, use it or lose it! Keep the association between your symbol or word or image and your response active and alive by making it a regular part of your sport psych repertoire. If you leave it unused for a while, don't forget to grease the wheels a bit with some practice and application so that it will work as well as it did previously.

Chapter Four

Mental Rehearsal:
New Twists on an Old Story

IN THE YEAR 1912, the American track and field star Jim Thorpe was traveling by ocean liner to Stockholm to compete in the Olympic Games. His teammates were practicing their respective events on a cork track aboard the ship when a reporter approached Thorpe, who seemed to be dozing in a lounge chair on deck. "What are you doing?" the reporter inquired, "I'm practicing the broad jump," Thorpe replied. "I just jumped twenty-three feet, eight inches." Thorpe continued with his method of training even after arriving in Sweden, exchanging the deck chair for a hammock. His regimen worked. Thorpe virtually dominated the games, finishing first in the decathlon and the pentathlon, fourth in the high jump, and seventh in the broad jump.

This little vignette reminds us that there is a lot more riding to be done than the hour or so every day or every few days that most people physically manage. Too many of us forget about the riding rings, indoor arenas, trails, or fields that can be constructed by our mind's eye. Great amounts of self-training can be accomplished while you are off your horse's back, away from the barn, and without wearing a stitch of britch.

What Is Mental Rehearsal?

Most riders, as well as other athletes, are already familiar with the term *mental rehearsal.* They understand it as a way of practicing or performing some athletic feat or activity through their imagination. Most associate it or even equate it with the process of visualization, but it is quite different from that; visualization is just one facet of mental rehearsal. A good mental rehearsal involves not only the visual senses, but hearing and taste and smell and feel and touch—the whole experiential shebang. Through the technique of mental rehearsal, riders can imagine the full experience of being on a horse's back, be it at a sitting trot and feeling their seat bones engaging, or shortening their horse's stride down a steady line and feeling their fingers close and their shoulders open ever so slightly, or asking for a haunches-in and feeling the arc of that inside bend in their leg and seat. They'll hear the regular, dull flap of the bell boots, or hear the footing being kicked up against the wall of the indoor ring, or feel a rhythm to their mental ride, or maybe smell hay, leather, liniment, sweat.

On the whole, mental rehearsal is a psychological technique that riders can use to imagine themselves riding in exacting, sensory detail for the purpose of changing or enhancing their attitudes, thoughts, feelings, or performance. It can also be used to practice technique, to condition oneself to respond in a certain way to stimuli in the environment, to analyze and correct errors in one's riding, and to prepare mentally for competition. It is not just riding mentally for the sake of getting in an extra ride per week, nor is it only the ideal ride or riding performance played over and over in one's imagination. It's a tool for making things happen differently in real life, and happen better.

How Does Mental Rehearsal Work to Effect Changes?

In 1983 two sport psychologists studied the effects of mental practice on sport performance. In their report, they discussed three possible explanations for a mental sensory experience actually changing one's ability. (1) The **symbolic learning theory** suggests that movements made in the head are symbolic of the physical movements made by the athlete, and because of this symbolism, there is a transfer of learning from the mental to the physical. (2) The **psychoneuromuscular theory** suggests that mental practice produces small muscle contractions that are similar to the contractions that occur during actual physical practice, although they are much smaller in scale. (3) The **motivational theory** suggests that the generalized muscular activity associated with mental practice results in a state of physical arousal that is good for athletic performance. That is, it's not the specific, technical riding movements that make a difference as much as the state of readiness that results.

Another idea proposed by sport psychologists for the success of mental rehearsal has to do with the concept of "overlearning." Physical movements or even emotional reactions that are practiced over and over again become automatic, less in need of conscious direction. Overlearning can prevent performances from being disrupted by anxiety in pressure situations; a person learns to rely on his or her "automatic pilot." This can happen with mental practice as well as through real life practice.

Who Should Use Mental Rehearsal?

- Anyone who wishes to "ride" more frequently than he or she has time for!

- Anyone with a bad riding habit who is having difficulty changing the habit while actually riding.

- Anyone who enjoys "reliving" lessons or special rides over in the mind. This is a very good way to "stamp in" and consolidate some new learning, experience, or technique.

Suffering from a Poor Reputation: What Mental Rehearsal Is Not

A lot of people stay away from mental rehearsal because of what they've heard or been taught about it. Given much of what I've heard and read, I can't blame them. Here are the more common misconceptions:

1. That you need to set aside a fifteen- or thirty-minute period to do it.

2. That you have to do it sitting down.

3. That you need quiet.

4. That it's good only for imagining the perfect trip or ride.

5. That you have to be a "good" visualizer.

All right; let's get rid of those one by one.

#1 Sport Psychology on the Go!

I don't know too many people who have an extra fifteen or thirty minutes in the day to prepare for their sport or hobby. And where time does free up, most people I know, myself included, immediately parlay it into getting another load of laundry done, or knocking off another errand, or into reading an extra story to a little one around the house. Time management is the name of everyone's game these days.

So forget all those things you heard about needing time to rehearse something in your head. I do my mental rehearsals while cleaning my tack, walking over to the mounting block, folding my laundry, waiting for the traffic light to turn green, brushing my teeth. Really, you don't need an entire mental video of performances; you just need a few frames. Five frames of a good half halt. Seven frames of coming forward to water. Do it again if you have time. Do it later if you don't. Six frames of saying *whoa* softly the moment you feel the horse tense up. Do it over and over, a little flicker of mental rehearsal throughout the day or week, so that it becomes a conditioned response in real life: *horse tenses—you say whoa.* Automatic. Just like that.

#2 If I'm Sitting Down, I'm Already Busy

The only time I sit down these days is to work, tie my field boots, or eat. I imagine it's much the same for others. If I have more time to sit down during the day or evening, you can be sure that I am watching a nice movie with my husband or playing a rousing game of Candyland with my sons. But as I explained in the section above, mental rehearsal can be designed for people on the go. If you can think on your feet, you can rehearse on them, too.

#3 Quiet? Where?!

The only time I'm aware of the quiet are the few moments before I drift off to sleep, and, for the most part, I don't care to do much work at that point. I think that others who are busy share my feelings. But think about how much productive thinking any of us gets done during the course of a normal day, with all its noises and activities going on around us; somehow we manage to keep from being too distracted to plan a meal, make a mental list, or think over a problem from work. I believe that anyone can talk himself or herself into "needing" quiet, but there probably are a lot of things we think we need quiet for that in fact we don't. One of these things may be mental rehearsal.

#4 Why Do You Think They Call It Rehearsal?

This is practice time, not fairy tale time. Use mental rehearsal to practice in your mind what you want to do differently or do better. If you hang back and pick at your horse's mouth coming down to square oxers, then practice keeping your hands quiet and your leg active as you imagine riding to different-looking square oxers. Desensitize yourself to them so that they are no longer a trigger for anxiety. Learn to develop a feel for the desired response. And once you've developed that feel, rehearse it again and again.

There are basically two ways in which mental rehearsal will work for you. One is, as its name suggests, that practice makes (or at least helps you approach) perfect. Mental rehearsal moves people toward improvements in the actual execution of movements, reactions, and mental skills. Second, the memory of specific action or sequence of actions can serve as a *reference experience* for you—one more mental resource—that you can draw on while you are riding and beginning to feel confused or stuck in a negative response or habit. What you want to develop is the capacity to use this rehearsed mental flash of riding experience to reorient you to the correct response or feel when you are riding and things aren't going well but you don't have time to think out what you want to change. You will use this mental rehearsal much as a sailor lost in a channel relies on the lighthouse to stay oriented to shore. At this juncture, mental rehearsal functions like the mental symbols and pictures described in the chapter on ideomotor training. Reference experiences also make excellent reset buttons, along with your slogans and symbols. Use them to set you right again when you've lost the sense of what you want from your body or from your horse. The difference between reference experiences and mental rehearsal is that reference experiences are based on your memories of an actual riding experience, and are more "condensed" versions of riding than are the imaginary snippets you rehearse.

People using mental rehearsal just for imagining their perfect performance in a global, nonspecific manner lose out on much of what the technique has to offer. See how the runners below used mental rehearsal to practice races run under less than ideal conditions:

> *Right before a big race, I'll picture myself running and I'll try and put all the other people from the race in my mind. I try to picture every possible situation that I find myself in . . . behind someone, boxed in, being pushed, different positions, laps to go, and of course the final stretch. And I always picture myself winning the race—no matter what! If I picture myself losing, I automatically erase that out of my mind!*

—Vicki Huber, a 3000-meter Olympic athlete

> *Hot weather is always difficult for me. So visualizing running in hot, humid conditions is an important part of my training. I just visualize it being hot—and not feeling warm. My technique is to image the absolute worst case scenario and then respond positively to it.*

—Nancy Ditz, Olympic marathoner

Remember that when Ditz talks about imagining the worst possible scenarios she's not talking about imagining tripping or getting a cramp. She's talking about the variables of conditions that she may have to run under, not the range of problems that could crop up. Therefore, you don't want to start thinking about your horse tripping and falling, or you doing a crash and burn on the hunt field, but perhaps it would be useful to rehearse in your head riding under muddy conditions or when your horse is a little fresher than usual.

#5 "What If I'm Not a Good Visualizer?"

Too many people have been taught to use mental rehearsal by imagining a flowing round or the seamless dressage test to which they have been aspiring and trying to hold on to those images when they go into the competition ring or arena. This works for some riders, either because they've gained some degree of confidence through the mental experience, or they use the experience to "oil" the body so that the relevant physical movements and mental processes are in place, or because they are able to use the images as internal orienting points for body position or pace. But it doesn't work for everyone. These other people lose the images by the time they are riding, or in the hubbub of the warm-up. For others, the rehearsed ride simply doesn't transfer over to any kind of change in their riding. And for yet uncounted others, visualizing something is just not their thing. It doesn't come easily, nor has it proved useful for improving how they ride or how they feel about their riding.

People's different sensory system preferences follow them into their recreational and sporting life. Some have enlivened auditory senses, and love the world of sound. They may prefer a concert to a movie or a play, remember more from an audiotaped lecture than from the same material offered in a magazine article. They speak in terms of *listening* to their horses or *hearing* what their instructors are saying rather than *sensing* what their horses are doing or *seeing* just what their instructors mean. The internal riding experiences of people who orient to their auditory senses and of those who orient toward the kinesthetic (feeling) or visual senses are as enriched and as valid as each other; they are just different.

Unfortunately, a lot of people have the mistaken idea that if you are not a good visualizer, then you can't benefit from mental rehearsal techniques. Baloney. The visual senses do not have any kind of lock on this technique. You can ride blind in your mind, immersing yourself in feeling or perhaps even just hearing yourself ride. For instance, try letting yourself imagine *feeling* your horse respond to your signal to walk on from a halt. Conduct mental test trials of your application of aids until you come upon the memory of that combination of hand, seat, and leg pressures that proved most effective. Then absorb yourself in the physical memory of that balance of aids so that it can become increasingly familiar and increasingly replicable.

Furthermore, visualizing isn't even relevant when it comes to practicing *attitude*. Mental rehearsal should never be limited to the practice of physical motions; it should also be used to rehearse getting and keeping that just-right mind set. Think back to a time or a ride when you felt great inside your head. The emotion could have been one of elation or relaxation or confidence or boldness or devil-may-care or aplomb. The important thing is that you can remember it and use it to guide your efforts to find it again. Practice drawing on your memory reserves and rehearsing the whole inner experience of that feeling or attitude or mind set.

Some People's Stories

Denise

Denise is that jumper rider who picks her horse's mouth to death whenever she comes down to a combination. She loses her eye, her horse loses his rhythm, and they both lose their confidence. Doubles, triples, in-and-outs—it doesn't matter. If there is more than one fence to be jumped in a row, her hands just start going. And going. By this time, they have developed dancing, nipping, jerking, pulling lives of their own and pay no heed to Denise's conscious and most effortful attempts to get them to knock it off. Her hands laugh at her and scurry around some more. Her horse groans.

Denise decides to do some mental rehearsal. She selects for practice the point in her ride when she first turns for her approach to an imaginary combination, up through the point of a few strides after she lands following the last element. And in her rehearsals she gradually begins to change what has been her customary response. She practices what it would feel like to do nothing with her hands for a few moments as she rounds her turn. This is the place where she usually begins to get unnecessarily active with her hands. And she practices that "do nothing" feeling a few times. She becomes aware, during her rehearsal, that she is a little nervous about doing nothing, because she has always thought that she didn't do *something*, she would feel that she had lost control. So she practices this experience in her mind and recognizes that doing nothing for a few strides isn't going to bring on the riding horrors that, over the years, she's talked herself into believing would happen—such as, for instance, her horse running off with her, her horse jumping out of the ring with her, her horse opening up to a "nineteen-foot stride" (remember, we are not rational beings when nervous!). And so maybe she does it a few more times before realizing that she has successfully desensitized herself to her anxiety about doing nothing with her hands.

Denise's next step is carrying the mental rehearsal a couple of frames further, maybe to where she's actually cantering down a few strides out from the first fence of the combination. And because doing nothing may not be the idea response here, Denise begins to practice maintaining a feel for her horse's mouth—supportive, elastic, communicative. She practices this in brief flashes of imagination—in as much time as it takes to do it in real life—while pouring her cereal in the morning or having a commercial interrupt her television program. Denise sometimes likes to slow down her rehearsals so that it rides in her mind like a slow-motion movie. This allows her to get a feel for what her hands need to be doing differently in order to get a better response from her equine partner. Pretty soon, the new image for riding down to combinations begins to supplant the old "picky" one in her mind and, gradually, in her body as well. Achieving begins with conceiving. Get the right idea in your mind, and the transfer to action becomes a natural next step.

Nathan

Nathan had an awful spook of a trail horse. His goal for using mental rehearsal was to develop a deeper, less reactive seat in response to his horse's shenanigans. He had not found useful the perched-over-the-neck and heels-in-the-air position he adopted in the months since he got Willie. It used to be that Nathan popped up on Willie's neck only after Willie had found something worthy to spook at, but now he does it in anticipation, whenever he even thinks Willie is going to do something. Of course, by now Willie has learned that whenever his rider pops up on his neck, "something" should happen, and so, being eager to please, he makes sure it does!

So Nathan rehearses the process of becoming a beanbag chair. In his mind, he hacks in fields, on trails, by roadsides, past pastures of cows—and imagines over and over the transformation of his nervous and stiff body into a heavy, sodden, shapeless beanbag chair. Sometimes it's the red vinyl ones of the 1970s that filled his first apartment as a graduate student, while others are modern spinoffs. And again and again in his mind Nathan plays out scenarios of Willie jigging and jogging and scooting this way and that, but instead of perching Nathan rehearses getting soft and heavy. He practices it all over again until it becomes such second nature to him that when he is on his horse and has even an inkling of his nervous response, what he does instead is become a big, soft, heavy beanbag chair. And because that is just what he has been mentally practicing, that is what begins to happen. For Nathan, the results reinforce themselves. As he discovers his capacity to respond differently, he becomes less anxious from the beginning of the ride; Willie, then, starts off more relaxed, too, reducing the pull for Nathan to respond by perching over his neck. Everybody's happier.

Shelly

Shelly has always had difficulty making the transition from the warm-up area to the dressage arena for her First Level tests. As soon as she hears the warning bell, she loses any confidence she has developed during her warm-up and begins to feel inadequate compared with the other competitors. That her feeling has nothing to do with reality is totally irrelevant. Good as she is, Shelly shrinks into her body and rides timidly into the arena.

Rather than run the "perfect" test through her mind over and over, Shelly has learned to use mental rehearsal specifically to improve her entrance. Starting from the moment that she finishes her warm-up, Shelly mentally goes through her experience of feeling composed and confident, and of having enjoyed, or at least having felt content with, how her horse was going, on to hearing the bell. At this point in her rehearsal, though, she imagines having a different response to the bell, or better yet, no response to it; it just becomes the sound that tells her it is time to walk up to the arena. By living over and over in her mind the sound of the bell, Shelly manages successfully to desensitize herself to it. Stripped of its "special" meaning, the warning bell becomes simply another noise telling her where to go when. Eventually, as her skills with mental self-training get better, Shelly is able to change the meaning of the bell altogether so that it becomes her personal trigger to drop into a profound state of concentration and composure.

But the rehearsal doesn't stop there. Shelly mentally practices riding right into that arena boldly, self-assuredly. She practices feeling as if she and her horse are absolutely brilliant. She trots in again and again in her mind, each time with a more elegant self-carriage, with a deeper seat, with better pace. Gradually this begins to supplant her memories of coming into arenas with her upper body collapsed over the pommel, her hands halfway up her horse's neck, and a backward, overcollected rhythm. This becomes both a new and reconstructed memory of her rides, so to speak, as well as a positive and powerful reference point for future ones. It starts to feel so vivid and real that the distinction is no longer clear between what has been imagined and what has been the real-life ride. Bingo.

What Else Can You Do with Mental Rehearsal?

Here are some other ways that riders can use mental rehearsal techniques:

- Rehearse specific technical riding skills, such as your half halts, the tactful use of spurs, staying off your horse's back long enough in the air over oxers, remembering to breathe, and so on.

- Rehearse a relaxation response to specific situations that have caused you to become anxious—crossing streams, coming down to a fence a half-stride off, your horse shying, getting called back for an equitation workoff.

- Rehearse getting rid of negative thoughts. Discover what works for you (i.e., imagine seeing and then erasing the negative thought off a blackboard; swat negative thoughts away with a fly swatter; call upon a team of mental "bouncers" in

your head that whisk the bad thoughts off to "thought jail";
say *later* to the thoughts; strike a deal with them to leave now
and come back only after the lesson or round or show or clinic
is over). Once you have one or two working tools, practice
using them at critical points so that you become facile at whatever mental gymnastics enables you to alter the immediate
contents of your mind.

• Rehearse applying different aids to "see" or "feel" how each
may make a difference in your ride. For instance, try using a
softer versus a firmer half-halt prior to your canter departs;
experiment with riding in as opposed to out of your tack,
while jumping, to figure out which way your horse goes better;
try asking for a bend versus a counterbend to distract your
horse from fiddling with his head and looking at the horses
turned out in the field while you ride.

• Rehearse a counterresponse to one that hasn't been working
very well. For instance, mentally practice opening your upper
body around turns (instead of hunching over), or keeping
your eyes up when your horse gets skittish or searches the
ground for bogeymen (instead of looking along with him), or
saying *whoa* and sighing to relax when your horse gets strong
with you (instead of yelling *stop it!* or shortening the reins by a
foot or so).

• Project yourself into the future and rehearse your riding skills
as if you are the rider you will be six months, one year, three
years from now. This strategy combines mental rehearsal with
the powerful psychological technique of future progression,
which allows people to see or, better yet, to experience themselves in the future. You can also use this technique to
rehearse your riding skills as if you were another rider whose
style you admire. Acting *as if* is different from imitating. Imita-
tion usually leads people to try to copy the physical "look" of
the admired style. This results in the imitator's looking or
feeling stiff and stylized without benefit of the underlying effectiveness. What you're really seeking here is an overall *as if*
feeling, not located specifically in body or mind but somehow

in both simultaneously. From that *as if* center, or core, radiates a wisdom of attitude and body movement that more closely approaches the ideal. It's like having had a little bit of a brain transplant from the admired rider, and you don't know exactly how it will affect you, only that it will.

The following is a terrific little vignette from the book *Thinking Body, Doing Mind: Tao Sports for Extraordinary Performance in Athletics, Business and Life* (Huang & Lynch, 1992), describing one athlete's use of the *as if* technique made even more powerful by its being combined with the use of a personal symbol (see Chapter 3, Ideomotor Training):

> *Vince Stroth, an offensive guard with the NFL's Houston Oilers, once came to me in order to improve his mental game. I asked him how he desired to play each game. He replied, "I want to be consistently alert and 'on top' of each down; to be persistent, 'dig in' and keep the pressure on; to never go away and to make my presence always felt." I suggested to him that this sounded like a description of an animal—actually, like a badger. Vince got excited as I told him to act "as if" he were a mean, wild badger. The very next game against the Los Angeles Raiders, Vince the Badger played in a way that is rarely matched by anyone at his position, culminating when he played a major role in two scoring drives.*

• Rehearse generating a sense of familiarity with a new physical setting that you will be exposed to and could become nervous about. For instance, in your mind go through what it would feel and look like going on that new trail, competing on the new showgrounds, riding in a group along that wooded path, or walking around the new indoor. Of course, this works best if you've already scouted out the place and have a real idea of what it will be like, but you can still get a lot of mileage out of making up the new surroundings. Fact and reality are less important in having this work for you than is having the mental experience of having ridden in a (any) new place and becoming mentally acclimated to that idea and not necessarily that specific place.

One of my all-time favorite sport psychology stories is of the

Soviet team preparing for the 1976 Summer Olympic Games in Montreal. They sent over representatives to photograph the facilities where the different events were going to be held. When the representatives returned to the Soviet Union, the photographs were studied by the athletes, who familiarized themselves with the pictures of the physical environment to create images of themselves performing there. Brilliant! By doing this, they obviated, or at least reduced, the disorientation that typically comes with being in novel surroundings. What a terrific way to help athletes feel acclimated, as if they have been there before, doing their thing all along.

Looking Out or Looking At—Which Is Better?

Riders often ask whether it is better to imagine themselves from the perspective of being in their own bodies, looking out, or whether it is better to imagine watching themselves, as if they were spectators. The first way is an internal perspective; the second way, an external perspective. The internal perspective most closely approximates the real-life mental and physical experience we have while riding, and because of that I recommend it as the preferred mode of doing mental rehearsal. Studies have shown, too, that successful athletes report a higher frequency of internal, as opposed to external, rehearsal experiences.

I always encourage riders, however, to do what works well for them. If they have been rehearsing from the perspective of watching themselves ride and have had good results with that, I suggest they continue. They may want to give the other way a try, but if it ain't broke, don't fix it. They should do what is comfortable for them.

Points to Remember

- Use all your senses in your rehearsals in order to make the experience as vivid and as real as possible. Smell the Vetrolin, hear your saddle leather squeak, feel the rubber nubs of the reins.

- Treat your imagination as you would a developing muscle. Use it regularly. Keep it "fit."

- About 98 percent (!) of top divers, hockey players, swimmers, and gymnasts use some form of imagery in their preparation and training. Why shouldn't you?

Chapter Five

Hypnosis and Self-Hypnosis: What's Truth, What's Myth, and What's It All Got to Do with Riding Horses?

The Real Scoop on Hypnosis

Hypnosis is probably one of the most misunderstood psychological phenomena around. Though it is often associated with the shenanigans seen on the entertainment stage, the hypnosis used in medicine, psychology, and dentistry is an altogether different thing; in fact, I don't consider the stage stuff hypnosis at all. "Stage hypnosis" is usually more a function of charismatic, authoritarian entertainers capitalizing on the extroverted, fun-seeking mood of audiences than it is a reflection of what real hypnosis is about. The bottom line is that hypnosis is no more a toy than are the other tools of the healing professions.

Clinical hypnosis, on the other hand, is not loud or brash, is not something that should take place at anyone's expense, is benign and subtle and powerful and sublime. It is a natural psychological experience, one that many people first experiencing it commonly recognize as familiar to them from ordinary experience. When put to use in specific settings and with a specific purpose by trained and ethical practitioners, hypnosis can facilitate change in a person's thoughts, feelings, perspectives, attitudes, sensations, or behaviors. These changes can be momentary or enduring, depending on the needs and wishes of the hypnotic subject or client and the skill of the physician, psychotherapist, or dentist.

There are many definitions of hypnosis, and each one stresses a different aspect of the hypnotic experience. I describe it as an altered psychological state of internally focused awareness, where the individual becomes absorbed in his or her own thoughts, ideas, physical sensations, or memories. This hypnotic state is typically accompanied by certain physiological changes, such as slowed breath rate, increased muscle relaxation, lowered blood pressure, and slowed pulse rate. Hypnosis allows the individual a modest or profound liberation from old and limiting ideas, frames of reference, and belief patterns, and permits receptivity to new and better—certainly more useful—mental patterns. It also allows the person to go deep inside himself or herself and reconnect or become familiar with lost, hidden, or latent aspects of personality that can help in solving a problem or improving a situation.

Hypnosis is not the same as sleep, nor it is a state where you suffer any loss of control. You cannot be "made" to do anything that you don't want to do, and you cannot be hypnotized if you don't wish to be. You also cannot get "stuck" in hypnosis, inasmuch as it is a cooperative, interactive process between professional and client, in which the client maintains as much awareness as he or she cares to. When the person's had enough, he simply decides so, opens his eyes, and lets the hypnotic experience dissipate. In fact, first-timers are often surprised at how easy hypnosis is to achieve and at how familiar it seems. They're also surprised at how much they remain aware of their surroundings, of what's being said to them, and of what they experience. Comments from clients of mine after they have experienced hypnosis for the first time in a session include:

- "This was really relaxing."
- "I was surprised that I could do it."
- "I can't believe how easy it was!"
- "It reminds me a little of when I used to meditate."
- "I got so into the feeling of actually riding that I hardly heard a word you were saying!"

- "Great color show . . . I was seeing all this blue—a beautiful indigo."
- "Pretty cool!"

Who Should Use Hypnosis or Self-Hypnosis?

- Anyone who enjoys indulging his or her imagination.
- Anyone who has enjoyed or made constructive use of his or her inner mental life.
- Anyone who's curious about it.
- Anyone else!

How Hypnosis Works

Hypnosis initiates change by creating a psychological environment where the hypnotized subject both becomes open to new ideas and suggestions and gains access to untapped mental resources. Let me explain these further.

Greater Receptivity to Suggestions and Ideas

Rather than being a ritualized, static procedure, in which a hypnotherapist "puts someone under," sound clinical hypnosis is better described as an exchange of communication between two people. During the process, the hypnotized subject becomes exposed, and more receptive, to new ideas and to cognitive and emotional experiences. These ideas and experiences can be old ones or recent ones or just promises of things to come. They can be prompted either by what the therapist says, or by the train of thoughts and memories generated within the hypnotized person.

Most people think of hypnosis primarily as a vehicle to mental and physical relaxation. That's a fine way to think of it, but is really only the beginning. Hypnosis can offer a person contact with a far wider sweep of serviceable psychological, physiological, and physical experiences than just relaxation; in fact, in my work with rider clients I often consider relaxation from hypnosis a serendipitous side effect of the work we are doing and rarely the major thrust, unless it has been specifically requested.

In any event, these new ideas or concepts, if they are relevant and appealing to the person, seep into the psyche, resulting in psychological or behavioral changes. The changes take place without the overly directed and effortful manner of most riders' previous attempts to improve their riding.

Let me give you an example of how a benign, therapeutic idea or word reverberating in one's mind can result in change. Several years ago my husband and I were conducting a workshop on hypnosis and psychotherapy for a group of therapists in the counseling psychology graduate program of a local university. We invited a member of the audience to be our demonstration subject for a brief single hypnotherapy session, which we would conduct for educational purposes in front of the group. Lilly volunteered, saying that she'd like to work on her excessive consumption of caffeine.

John and I then had a short interview with Lilly in front of the group in order to find out how she used caffeine in her life and to determine how we could help her comfortably decrease her intake. After twenty minutes or so of discussing how we could help Lilly "decaffeinate" her life, we all broke for lunch.

When we returned an hour later, I strolled to the back of the conference room before starting and helped myself to some tea and cookies provided by the university. I have always drunk regular caffeinated tea, so imagine my surprise when, fifteen minutes later, in the middle of the hypnotic session, I looked down at my Styrofoam cup and realized that I had inadvertently selected a decaffeinated teabag! I always think of that if I need a reminder of the power of subliminal suggestion.

Now, imagine if, rather than *decaffeinated,* the concept of *soft* or *fluid* or *rhythmic* or *decisive* or *patient* were to be suggested to a rider during hypnosis. Again, the idea could be prompted by the therapist or the client herself. Many of my clients select their words. I then incorporate them into the hypnosis we are doing, or the client suggests the word or words to herself during hypnosis sessions in the office, or during self-hypnosis sessions at home. The key is to capitalize on the ability of the hypnotic state to subconsciously influence thought, feeling, or action in effortless ways, so that the old bugaboos of trying too hard (and ruining everything) are eliminated.

Gaining Access to Inner Mental Resources

The other useful attribute of hypnosis is its ability to reconnect a person with lost or hidden psychological "talents," the various hypnotic phenomena that an individual comes by naturally, or other mental qualities with which he or she has lost touch.

Let's say, for example, that you used to be a bold, decisive rider who would tell your combined training horse, *"Go forward now, and open up your stride because you are jumping this picnic table no ifs ands or buts, now let's go!"* But maybe something happened to shake your confidence or maybe you took a year off to have a baby and when you came back to riding you just couldn't get there again. To your dismay—or horror—you find yourself saying to your horse, *"Hey, guy, I think this would be a good time to open up a little and would you please keep going forward and I'd really be grateful if you got us over this fence and I promise I'll give you a lot of carrots OK what do you say there?"* And you go home and say to yourself, *"whatever happened to me?"*

This is a perfect opportunity to use hypnosis. With it, you can go back a little in time (a month, a year) and experientially return to that mental or psychological frame of mind that used to give you the riding confidence and daring you now miss. Once there, you "walk around," reacquainting yourself with that memory, recalling what it felt like, what you felt like with it, the kinds of things you'd have said to yourself while on course, the kinds of mental prep you'd have done, and so on. And then you bring it back with you to the here and now. You see, it never really left you; it was only lost somewhere, either because of an event that severed the connection (like a fall), or because you were away from the sport for an extended period of time (for pregnancy or work and family demands), or because of some gradual erosion of confidence (a string of disheartening lessons, worries about becoming disabled from injury, riding a poorly schooled horse for a while).

One client of mine, having lost her confidence about going fast on horseback, "galloped" during one of her first hypnosis sessions. Roxie came out of the experience simply awestruck. Laughing and crying at the same time, she said, "My God, it was so real! I had forgotten how much I missed doing that!'' Having reconnected to this seemingly lost part of her, Roxie was able to bring the enthusiasm and confidence back to her riding again.

In sum, the effectiveness of hypnosis is based on the idea that people have many talents or resources that have been kept hidden from view or from use by anxiety, trauma, outmoded thoughts, old frames of reference, outdated self-concepts, and other psychological obstacles. Hypnosis can mobilize these resources and make them accessible. The person can then use the resources to consciously or subconsciously generate the attitudes, feelings, mindsets, physical sensations, and behaviors that can facilitate his or her achievement of personal or athletic goals.

The Physiological Signs of Hypnosis

There are a variety of physiological reactions that the body commonly manifests during the hypnotic state. Sometimes people experience a few one time, and different reactions during another session. I welcome these signs in a client, because they let me know that something is beginning to happen. They also validate the client's experience that something different is indeed happening, especially if it's one of the first times the person has been hypnotized and isn't sure whether he or she is feeling the hypnosis. The following are the more commonly experienced body reactions:

- Slowed breathing rate (although some people, especially first-time hypnosis clients, may experience their breathing rate becoming quicker before it slows).

- Lowered pulse rate and blood pressure (typically inferred, as few individuals can actually directly tell that these have taken place).

- Muscular relaxation.

- Changes in the swallow and blink reflexes (both become less frequent).

- Dampening of the startle response (you orient and startle less in response to unexpected movement or sound).

- Changes in eye behavior:
  eyes defocus
  eyes tear lightly
  eyelids flutter (rare, as most people prefer to have their eyes closed during hypnosis anyway).

The Psychological and Subjective Signs of Hypnosis

There are other, more psychological and subjective changes that take place during hypnosis. Collectively called the constellation of hypnotic phenomena, these changes are the foundation experiences from which clients can modify their behavior, thinking patterns, attitudes, and feelings. These hypnotic phenomena—the natural behavioral and experiential byproducts of hypnosis—are such subjectively experienced psychological events as remembering, forgetting, changes in one's sense of time passage, and perceptual alterations. Listed below are some of the more commonly experienced hypnotic phenomena and a brief description of how they can be used in equestrian sport psychology:

a. *A desire not to move much during the hypnotic experience.* Known in professional circles as *catalepsy,* this phenomenon is most often experienced as a pleasant sense of body quiet or peacefulness. Sometimes people describe the feeling as a heaviness or even a numbness, like what novocaine induces. The feeling can be applied in situations where a rider gets too busy with her hands, body, or weight shifts, or where anxiety causes nervous tremors, knotted stomach, and the like. Catalepsy, by the way, is also a tool for helping people manage difficult medical procedures where movement is counterproductive, such as MRIs, amniocentesis, splinter removal, and so forth.

b. *Alterations in one's sense of time passage.* With this hypnotic phenomenon, you feel time going by either much more slowly than it actually is going (called *time expansion*), or more quickly than it actually is going (*time contraction*). In the first condition, ten minutes of hypnosis will feel like fifteen or twenty, and in the second, twenty minutes of hypnosis will feel like five or ten. I use this phenomenon of time distortion a lot with riders, teaching them to slow down their internal clocks so that they don't rush through their hunter rounds or dressage tests or figures. Think of how many times you have heard or have said yourself, "I went into the ring and picked up my canter, and the next thing you know my round was over and I don't remember a thing about what I did—it was all a flash." Time distortion techniques allow riders to feel as if they have all the time in the world to do the job ahead of them, which can make an enormous difference in how someone rides a round or a test.

c. *Forgetting.* Believe it or not, a little *amnesia* sometimes isn't such a bad thing. It can be very useful in helping people dissolve unwelcome memories of bad falls, or in helping people forget about, or "let go of," a sour experience with a trainer or client or horse. One of its best features is that it can make a break between past and present, between what happened then and what can happen now. I have helped riders use this technique to drive protective wedges between traumatic riding experiences and what the future holds in store for them.

d. *Enhanced memory.* Called *hypermnesia,* this is a good tool for those riders needing to reacquaint themselves with positive riding experiences from their stock of personal memories, or to remember the conditions (both psychological and environmental) that gave rise to good riding experiences.

e. *Future progression.* This is an ability to experientially project yourself into the future. It is useful for imagining yourself riding six months or one year from now, or even three years from now, with all the improvements learned along the way. Sometimes people find it helpful to "look back" during future progression and see what steps took them where they are, or, if they don't like where they imagine having ended up, they can reconsider their current and proposed courses of action. Future progression is always very helpful in creating a vision of the future for those riders who feel hopeless about change or progress.

f. *Age regression.* This is an ability to relive earlier experiences. It is the complement of future progression and is useful in reminding people of the way they used to think or feel or react as a rider, the way they liked but lost contact with. Age regression can help riders resurrect these hidden parts of themselves or at least remind themselves that they did (and therefore do) have those abilities or skills.

g. *Responsiveness to post-hypnotic suggestion.* This phenomenon allows people to be responsive to a suggestion, given earlier, at precisely the time when it really matters—at the show, in the starting box, when you first feel your horse getting antsy on the trail. An example of post-hypnotic suggestion is the following: *"The very moment you walk through that in-gate, your focus can become impenetrable."*

h. *Detachment from uncomfortable inner sensations or from anxiety-inducing external situations.* Often referred to as *dissociation,* this phenomenon is useful for disengaging temporarily from some emotional situation that threatens your ability to concentrate, remain composed, or otherwise perform to your best ability. Some riders find this useful when trying to ride, without being distracted, at a show where their ex-trainer is watching. Others use it to disengage for a few hours or for the day from worrisome problems at home or at school. It is frequently used by people suffering from chronic pain syndrome to get some respite from physical discomfort that can be safely ignored or overridden for periods of time.

Now that you're familiar with the varieties of hypnotic experience, read the following excerpts from hypnosis sessions I've conducted with equestrian clients to see how this applied to riding.

Using amnesia to help a rider get over a bad fall:

. . . I also recognize, from what you've told me already, Cathy, that you know about forgetting, but I don't know if you've ever thought of it helping you . . . It can help you . . . to forget about that fall, that whole miserable afternoon . . . We all forget things that have happened to us. I've forgotten what color jacket I wore to horse shows two summers ago, and you can go ahead and forget about that miserable day, let it go to oblivion as well as all the images and feelings and sounds associated with it, gone; it can recede, over time or all at once according to your preference . . . I wonder if you know all the ways in which memories recede . . . some go into hiding, others become irrelevant and so go on their way, others simply blur around the edges, get gray in the middle

until you've forgotten what it was to begin with and you are left with a clean slate upon which to sketch your future rides . . .

Using catalepsy to help a rider with too-busy hands:

. . . Perhaps already you're beginning to feel that quiet inside again, like the last time, and now maybe you can have it happen even more quickly, more quietly, feeling yourself become more and more still . . . hands very quiet, now and later—when you ride—when you ask your horse for something, quietly, effectively, softly, your horse will delight in your quiet hands . . . feel them resting so quietly in your lap? . . . You can borrow from this experience, you know, go ahead and take a "feeling snapshot" of it for later, for when you ride, so that you can really remember how easy and how pleasurable it is to feel your hands doing everything they need to be doing and no more . . . just enough . . . effective, simple, quiet . . .

Using future progression to help a rider feel less stuck in a riding rut:

. . . Take a moment to pick that time in the future you wish to visit . . . With each easy, slow breath you can find yourself that much closer to the right time. Maybe it's this coming summer, or maybe you prefer going ahead to a year from now to really see and feel and hear and experience everything you possibly can about what your riding will be like then . . . what you, Todd, as a rider will be like then . . . Invite your subconscious mind to help you select the time if you want, while you just sit there and enjoy the experience of hypnosis . . . and of wondering which image or which sounds of the future will present themselves to you, and when you'll know whether your subconscious chose this month or next, this year or next, to accomplish your goals [long pause] and once you're settled into a time that is comfortable for you just let me know, either by telling me or nodding or simply raising an index finger [long pause]. That's right . . . now that you've signaled me, why not take your time and ride around in that future self of yours and figure out what's different, what feels better, what was successfully changed, what still needs work . . . Can you feel yourself a different rider? . . . Good . . . Do you like what you feel? Is it OK? . . . Take all the time you want to ride this way so that when you've gone back to the present you can bring something of that riding with you . . . it can be a reference experience for you, a resource, a tool . . .

Using age regression to help a rider reconnect with her lost sense of confidence:

> . . . Now that you've gone back to visit yourself riding last year, why don't you take a moment to select just which memory will best serve you in reconnecting to your bravery, your boldness . . . You had it then . . . it didn't go anywhere far away, you know, just kind of got lost from you . . . It got spooked by all those stops and runouts . . . It can come back to you now . . . Slip that head set back on and really remember what it felt like . . . what it feels like now . . . and pick some kind of mental cue or trigger or symbol so that you can have it come back to you now whenever you want it to . . . make it yours again . . .

A New Kind of Hypnosis

Hypnosis has changed enormously in both use and delivery style over the past few decades. The old kind of hypnosis that most people are familiar with (from movies, television, and stage shows) is the authoritarian, autocratic version: "Your eyelids feel like lead weights, closing, closing . . ." and "Come morning, cigarettes will taste to you like chicken feed!" are characteristic of this type of stuff. This is such bad hypnosis that I can barely keep a straight face when I hear or read about it.

Enter the modern age of hypnosis. Techniques have become much more democratic, permissive, and personalized. In this newer context, hypnosis becomes a "joint venture" between therapist and client, with the client as collaborator in the work being done. Pioneered by renowned psychiatrist Milton H. Erickson (1901–1980), this gentler and more inviting hypnosis has gained, over the years, a strong following by those who recognize both its greater effectiveness and broader scope of application. Using language such as "You may feel some beginning sense of relaxation and comfort as your eyes close" and "I don't know whether you'll recognize changes today when you ride or sometime over the weekend," it allows the client to feel and be in control of what the hypnotic experience will be like, as well as of the how, where, and when of the change process itself.

Not only did Dr. Erickson distinguish clinical hypnosis from stage, thus legitimating its use in medical, dental, and psychological settings; he also departed radically from the traditional hypnosis by conceptualizing clients as active participants in the healing process rather than as passive recipients of a hypnotherapist's suggestions and ideas. The following are other departures from the old hypnosis that render this new form more appealing to both practitioner and subject:

Respect for the Individuality of the Person

Practitioners using this kind of orientation for their hypnotic work tailor the hypnosis specifically and carefully to the needs, interests, and personality style of the client. They educate themselves about the client's social and personal frames of reference to the world and about how they anticipate changing, and incorporate into the hypnosis those values deemed important by the client. It is never assumed that what worked for one client will automatically work for another; even if the problem or issue seems similar; two people may experience anxiety in very different ways, and the means by which they overcome it can be as different, too. This is dissimilar to the more standardized, cookbook-style delivery of hypnotic suggestion that is characteristic of some of the old-style hypnosis still going around.

Making Constructive Use of a Client's Personal Mental Resources

Rather than imposing foreign suggestions, ideas, and other curative measures onto a client, a hypnotherapist working in this newer tradition will try to "mine" for valuable experiences within the client that can be put to constructive use. In this way, the hypnosis never feels superficial but instead reflects a part of that person's inner life that can be corrective and restorative. If a rider has developed a problem of heavy, rigid hands and happens, by profession or hobby, to be a pianist, I will use her music experiences to help her in the riding. Using hypnosis to deepen her experience of imagining playing the piano during the session, I will ask her how she maintains that floating, light feeling in her hands and arms while she plays, and invite her to re-create the sensation right then, during the hypnosis. With lightness in hand (excuse the pun), I will then help her find ways to transfer that ability to her riding. She maintains light hands in one context; why not in the other? The ability to do that is present; it just needs to be made more accessible to this pianist-rider.

Flexible Induction Style That Allows for Each Person to Go into a Hypnotic Trance in His or Her Own Way

While old-style hypnotic inductions (that's the beginning part of the hypnosis, where the person gradually becomes hypnotized) tend to be pretty limited in range, those of this newer hypnosis are tailored to the individual. Therefore, imagery may play a large role in the induction for a client who is good at imagery, and not in that of someone who doesn't care for imagery. Some people become more easily absorbed by references to sounds, others to colors or ideas, and others to the subtle goings-on in their body. Some people experience hypnosis most comfortably when the hypnotherapist is very talkative during the induction; others like a quiet induction with lots of empty space to listen to their own thoughts. Good hypnotherapists take into account not primarily how they like to do hypnosis but how their clients can most effectively experience it. This takes a lot of the wind out of the argument that certain kinds of people "can't" be hypnotized. The more creative, flexible, and astute the hypnotherapist, the broader the range of clientele he or she can successfully work with.

Self-Hypnosis

Now that you have a good idea of what regular hypnosis is all about, here's some information about a kind of hypnosis that you can do by and to yourself. Occasionally referred to as *autohypnosis,* self-hypnosis is the process by which people develop a hypnotic state of internally focused awareness on their own. They can do with that experience any of the things described possible for hypnosis that is induced by a therapist. It is often easier for people to have satisfactory results from self-hypnosis *after* they've had some experience or training in being hypnotized by someone else. This way, they know what to expect from hypnosis and have a way of gauging if they're on the right track. Another variable determining people's success with self-hypnosis is how comfortable they are with fantasy. Those who don't tend toward much of that naturally, or who aren't comfortable with unstructured mental activities, will probably not have as rich an experience as those who indulge their imaginations regularly. Even those who do well with self-hypnosis, however, often say that the experience they have with it is not as deep or as rich as that with regular hypnosis. Nonetheless, it can be as effective, especially with practice. Here's how you do it:

✔ Start by sitting comfortably in a room without distractions.

✔ Allow ten or fifteen minutes for the first several times that you practice self-hypnosis. Eventually, you will be able to immerse yourself in the experience much more quickly and in many different settings, both quiet and active.

✔ Close your eyes and softly turn your attention to your breathing for an initial focus point. The self-induction of hypnosis can then begin with any of the following techniques, as well as with any mental techniques that get you to where you psychologically want to be:

1. **Diaphragmatic breathing:** Breathe in through your nose and out through your mouth. Exhale slowly. Use counting (one for in, two for out) if it helps you to regulate the rhythm. Allow your breathing to slow down and become more regular, rather than trying to make anything happen. The term *diaphragmatic* simply refers to using your diaphragm (in the abdomen) rather than just breathing in and out from your upper chest area. If you find yourself concentrating so hard on your breathing that it is making you less rather than more relaxed, just breathe as you would normally and try one of the other induction techniques.

2. **Staircase Induction:** This easy technique allows you to learn to self-hypnotize in a structured step-by-step (again, forgive the pun) fashion. Simply imagine yourself at the top of a staircase and begin to walk down. With each step down, ask yourself to become a little bit more immersed in the internal awareness state, which may or may not yet be hypnosis. Include in your experience the feel of any banister that is

part of your awareness (wood? metal?) or the feel of the steps (marble? carpeted?). Colors and sound will further serve to enrich your experience. Also, some people like to do this from atop a pyramid or mountain trail. Use your imagination to your own advantage.

3. **Counting Backward:** Some people are able to hypnotize themselves simply by counting backward, say from 50 or so down. Orient toward the lower numbers representing deeper levels of absorption. You can count back up at the end of the hypnosis as a means to gradually reorient to the external world.

✔ As your mind begins to wander during the self-induction techniques, simply allow it to do so. With self-hypnosis, there are no such things as distractions, just new directions of thought and sensation. If you wish, you can structure the experience a little more by selecting a particular image to start with. Some of the more popular are beaches, woods, and meadows. You can use them as "foundation" images, upon which you continue to build the hypnotic experience as your senses open up, or allow it to transform naturally to fit in where your mind has taken you. Nothing is static with hypnosis. As with dreams, everything is free to move, transform, and mutate, without (immediately apparent) rhyme or reason.

✔ When you wish, introduce an idea or image or memory or body sensation that has, or could have, some personal meaning for you and your riding. Examples are:

1. a memory of a good ride, where everything "clicked";

2. an image of yourself at the Zone Finals; completing your first endurance ride; riding a flawless dressage test; calming a spooked horse on her first trail ride;

3. a sensation of your body as light, centered, quiet, responsive, having independence of movement, or having depth of seat;

4. an experience of relaxation, inspiration, readiness, confidence, competence

✔ Find a mental motto or symbol that can be used to represent relevant, goal-promoting aspects of your hypnotic experience. Examples include:

1. a "kinesthetic snapshot" of that good ride or of a terrific, clean canter depart; the date of a special riding event where you felt great; the song you listened to driving home that day;

2. the name of the city where the Zone Finals or endurance ride will be held; a mental picture of an inspiring judge's card; the white britches of Grand Prix show jumping;

3. a triangle standing on its base (centered body); a still summer pond (quiet body); a marionette (independent, loose body movements); a rocket blasting off (aggressiveness, competitiveness); captain's hat (in charge and decisiveness); the color blue (staying cool).

"How Will I Know If I've Hypnotized Myself?"

• You will be internally absorbed by your thoughts, feelings, memories, body sensations, and like experiences.

• You may notice physiological changes, for example, slowed breathing rate or swallowing reflex, or muscular relaxation.

• You may notice changes in such physical sensations as warmth, coolness, lightness, or heaviness in your body or in just certain parts of your body (i.e., hands, legs).

• You may find yourself experiencing one or more of the hypnotic phenomena (tunnel vision, time distortion, hypermnesia, dissociation).

KEEP IN MIND . . .

✔ Practice is the key to the successful use of self-hypnosis. Like other mental skills, the ability to induce a hypnotic state in oneself must be developed over time. Try a schedule of practicing a few times each week for several weeks in a row. As your skill develops, you can expect the following to happen:

- You'll become absorbed into a hypnotic state, and in particular into your targeted mental experience, more and more quickly, eventually needing only a few moments to attain it.

- The hypnotic experience will become increasingly rich and vivid.

- You'll access the target experience in a wider variety of situations and settings, including those which are more anxiety-provoking (i.e., shows, lessons, events).

✔ The idea of using self-hypnosis is not only to absorb yourself in pleasant experiences when at home or at rest but to quickly resurrect mental resources just before or while riding. What you're looking to do is to train yourself to make quick forays into your mind, retrieve what you need (memory, symbol, feeling), and come back, all in an instant.

✔ Self-hypnosis capitalizes on the natural psychological phenomenon of ideomotor responding. As described in Chapter 3, this is the body's tendency to respond with physical activity to an idea. So, if you are thinking "centered," your body's tendency is to center itself. It is the same with thinking "soft" or "rhythmic" or any other thing. This is why it is important *not* to focus on negative thoughts or images, lest the body orient itself in precisely the wrong direction (thinking to oneself "I will not become tense" often leads to that very outcome).

These are the basics (and then some) of hypnosis and self-hypnosis. At this point, I hope the myths have been teased out of the reader's conceptions of these natural psychological experiences and replaced by an understanding not only of what they are truly about but also of how they can be constructive additions to a rider's repertoire of mental tools. Building on the power of self-suggestion and the making of new meanings to create new realities, the next chapter on rituals and symbols will add to the collection of tools and strategies that can enhance your riding.

Chapter Six

The Power of Ritual and Symbol in Riding

RITUALS AND SYMBOLS are regular and accepted parts of our everyday, non-riding lives. Formalized rituals such as weddings, commencements, bar mitzvahs, bon voyage parties, and baby showers all help us mark transitions from one phase of our lives to another, or embark on new adventures, be they spiritual, athletic, intellectual (i.e., going off to college), or otherwise. And rabbit feet, matchbooks from the wedding, pictures from a special party, the wrapping paper hat from the shower, as well as your morning mug are all symbols that represent, in condensed form, something worth remembering: a moment of personal history, a feeling, a state of mind, an event. Symbols are what you can take with you.

Rituals and symbols have long histories, having been around probably since the beginning of civilization, when groups of people had the need to highlight, punctuate, celebrate, or mourn changes in their lives. Rituals, in particular, serve as catalysts to transition—they carry you over the threshold into a different frame of mind, level of commitment, phase of development, or degree of mastery. They can also help you move past a point where you may have been stuck in your personal life or sport or work. Rituals can make the abstract and immaterial into something more concrete. They are surprisingly more powerful than people imagine, and can do wonderful things for your riding! It's the same for symbols, which make concrete an attitude or feeling and enable you to access it more easily by cueing it up. To the subconscious, the symbol is the whole thing.

Who Should Use Rituals and Symbols?

- Anyone who would like to mark, specifically and definitely, his or her progress with something memorable.

- Anyone who wants to move beyond a traumatic or disturbing event, such as a fall, a bad horse show, a death of a favorite horse, a break with a trainer.

- Anyone who, while riding, wants to learn how to change her mental set quickly from thinking the "wrong" thoughts or feeling the "wrong" feelings.

- Anyone who wants to celebrate a special event or development in his riding.

How Do I Use Rituals and Symbols to Help My Riding?

There are two ways in which you can put rituals and symbols to work for you. One is to use them as markers of progress, and the other is to use them to put some aspect of the past behind you. In the latter instance, a ritual works as a wedge between past and present, and a symbol keeps you connected to the present. Here are some examples of each:

Marking Progress . . .

. . . with a ritual

✔ *You're finally ready to move up from training level to novice after a long period of hard work. But letting go of what is safe and familiar is hard, and you feel nervous about your first event at the new level. So you decide to throw a "graduation ceremony" for yourself, to which you invite your trainer and a few friends from the barn who've witnessed*

*your progress. You arrive with pizza and sodas or a cake a few days
before the event, or the night before the event when everybody at the
barn is preparing.*

. . . with a symbol

✔ *You once avoided hacking out because you weren't sure you could cope
with what might happen, but that has changed over the last year as
you've gained confidence in yourself and a greater familiarity with
your horse. So you decide to take along that snapshot of you last
summer—the one where you're mounted up for a trail ride and look as
nervous as could be—and the one of you out on the trail just last week,
and laminate them together side by side. Up on the inside lid of your
tack trunk they go, your symbolic representation of the changes you
made, reminding you of these changes each and every time you go out
to ride.*

Putting the Past Behind You . . .

. . . with a ritual

✔ *You had a frightening and discouraging runaway two months ago
after your horse's martingale broke, and have been haunted by the
experience ever since. Use the power of ritual to bury—literally—the
memory and the accompanying haunting residue. You take a few days
to select the right location and to compose a guest list (trainer, spouse,
pet, barn buddy, the horse himself—or you choose to do it alone) and
you hold a funeral service for the event. You dig a hole, and with due
pomp and circumstance, bury that broken piece of martingale with all
of its memories of the incident. Done, goodbye, walk away.*

. . . with a symbol

✔ *You started off the new show season disastrously and were about to
give this sport the old heave ho when you finally pulled it all together
at one show in late June. You felt right, your horse felt right, the two of
you together felt right—all the hard work and learning crystallized*

*somewhere inside since your last outing, and it felt as if it was now
yours for the taking. So you take the cover page from the prize list of
this late June show and tuck it away inside your helmet as your private
personal symbol to ground you to this new rider you've become.*

Using a Concrete Symbol
to Effect a Change in Mind Set

There is a third way to utilize symbols to improve your riding, and that
is by selecting and keeping near you a concrete symbol (something
you actually can see, touch, or carry with you) that helps you quickly
shift your psychological mood or attitude. Different from a good luck
charm, this symbolic item has a distinct personal meaning to you that
may or may not be recognizable to others. I'll offer two case examples:

The Silver Bullet

Heidi was an amateur owner-jumper-rider who suffered a tempo-
rary loss of confidence after a difficult season with a new horse. She
longed to return to the way she used to feel on course, and especially
on jump-off courses, where she'd fly around the ring boldly, decisively,
confidently. She described this as her silver bullet state of mind—
sharp, aggressive, targeted.

Following one of our telephone sessions after a horse show at which
she'd choked during a jump-off, I suggested that Heidi, on returning
home, should go to a gun shop and purchase for herself a shiny new
silver bullet. She laughed, liking the idea for both its ritual and symbolic aspects. The bullet was to become her symbol, her concrete
representation of that aggressive, targeted, focused state of mind. It
was to be kept in the pocket of her britches when she showed, the
association between symbol and psychological set crystallized and
revalidated through the use of mental rehearsal, self-hypnosis, and
Heidi's own long-standing identification with the object itself.

King of Hearts

A client who had worked with me earlier on the goal of becoming more assertive with her strong-willed horse returned for consultation after her purchase of a new one. Wishing to start off on the right foot, letting this new horse know from the get-go who was boss, Gina and I discussed ways for her to keep active and strong her ability to assert her authority over the new charge. One of the things that came up during the consultation was Gina's need to have something to trigger this attitude within her once she got to the barn. Otherwise, she worried, she'd have difficulty resurrecting the feeling of being in charge, and she'd once again allow her horse to walk all over her both on the ground and while she was mounted.

Given Gina's affinity for things regal, and her wish to balance being authoritative with being compassionate, I suggested that she put on her new horse's stall door the king of hearts from a deck of cards. This way, as soon as she approached her horse for the day, she'd have a visual trigger for the mind set that had given her great success with her earlier horse, and that she knew she needed for her current riding goals and good relationship with her new buddy.

Creating Your Own Rituals and Symbols

Ask yourself the following questions in order to devise a personalized ritual that can help you move onto or solidify a new phase of riding development:

a) The Event

What is the accomplishment or transition that I want to celebrate or emphasize? Or, what is the experience or mental set that I want to put behind me?

b) The Ritual

What "rite of passage" would make me feel that the new development is now a reality? Do I want it to be festive? Solemn? Poignant? Funny?

c) The People

Who do I want to be there with me to share this ritual? Spouse, children, grandparent, trainer, barn buddy, maybe the horse? Perhaps it should be a private affair?

d) The Problem Symbol (Discarding It with a Ritual)

Is there something I wear or use that symbolizes the old me, something that I can give away or throw out? Old boots? Cheap tack? An old-fashioned jacket?

e) The Solution Symbol

Is there some article of clothing or equipment that represents this new way of being, thinking, feeling, riding? White britches? A fancy stall nameplate? Dress gloves?

Group Rituals

There are times when it is especially useful to do rituals in groups. The group can comprise people all from the same barn, family, or pony club. In such cases, the group decides together to do something to mark a special situation they are all experiencing together. Examples are the following:

- A family of riders does terribly at a horse show. Afterward, they can hardly say the name of the show without someone groaning and rolling his eyes over the day. So they decide once and for all to "get rid" of the experience. They take the one remaining prize list and, ferociously ripping it into little pieces, use it for kindling at the barbecue they decide to have on the eve of their next show.

- A barn is moving to a new facility. Mixed feelings abound; everyone agrees it's for the better, but there's something nice and familiar about the old place. The trainer and riders from the barn together decide to create a ritual around saying goodbye to the old place. They come up with the idea of signing a big balloon with all of their names and their favorite things or memories about the old place, and then, in a group, walking to one of the back fields and letting it go. They return to the barn for one last gathering in the tack room with doughnuts before starting the packing process.

I know of a trainer who did something like this on the other side of the transition. Naturally sensitive to the impact of change on people, and on kids especially, he rounded up all his younger riders and, one week before making the relatively abrupt move to a different facility in the middle of winter, brought them over to the new property. The kids ran around the place for hours, getting the lay of the land, exploring nooks and crannies, picking their stalls. Everyone felt better after that and was in a much better position emotionally to pack up the old place and make the move.

Group Symbols

Groups of people can utilize the same or similar symbols. The group aspect can lend an element of play to the situation, which automatically serves to reduce tension, fear, or worry about something that has happened or might happen. Let me give you an example of how I've worked with barns in which everyone had a bit of the show jitters.

I would arrive with a big Tupperware box full of colorful pipe cleaners and another full of beads, bells, and small pieces of polystyrene. Everyone from the barn was invited to make a "worry creature." They then assembled beaded, belled pipe-cleaner creatures, which looked something like the photo at left.

Now, don't for a moment think that it's only the kids who get into making worry creatures. I found this out the first time I ever did the exercise with a group. I had brought along a different, more "mature" exercise for the adults, thinking it would have greater appeal to them, but I realized my mistake when they took a dive for the brightest pipe cleaners and started immediately twisting and turning them into creatures, leaving the kids with all the poopy colors. You live and learn.

Anyway, the fun doesn't stop there. Everyone is encouraged now to give life to his worry creature by taking it home and talking to it, naming it, and bringing it back to the barn. They are instructed specifically to tell their creature their worries about riding—whether it's messing up at shows, being embarrassed at lessons, or worrying about flubbing the next team penning or horse trial. Then they trade their creatures (and, indirectly, their worries) for the day, or bury their creatures deep inside their tack trunks (along with the worry!), or toss them into a basket that the trainer has set up in the middle of the ring before each lesson to store everyone's distracting concerns. They can console their worry creatures, yell at them, send the whole bunch of them away anonymously to a rival barn! Everyone can choose a different strategy or can mix and match, or the barn can decide together to do one of the above as a group ritual, say, the last lesson day before the next show or trial or rodeo. The point is to break up, with a bit of whimsy, any tension associated with riding, as well as to discharge it through ritual and symbolic techniques that are eminently more powerful in the doing than one ever imagines in the reading. Do them and see!

Chapter Seven

Performance Anxiety Is One Thing, but What If I'm Really Scared?

FEAR, IN CONTRAST to performance anxiety or nervousness, is a different ballgame. Being afraid of getting maimed on horseback is different from being afraid that your peers will laugh at you for doing the wrong test or missing all eight spots to your fences.

There are probably few other popular sports where the risk of serious injury is so high. This is due, of course, to the nature of the activities involved (like jumping over picnic tables) and the variable of "the unpredictable" (like twelve-hundred pounds of spook and silliness). Even when you consider other sports like sky diving, motorboat racing, or downhill skiing, the risks involved are often more mechanical or physical in nature (speed, velocity, slope, density of snow or ice), and thus at least a little bit more predictable. And, when you think of it, there are few of these high-risk sports that draw women to them anywhere to the degree that riding does. So for women, the equestrian sports are usually the most dangerous activities in which they become involved.

Therefore, that people become fearful upon occasion during their riding career should come as no surprise. It's only a surprise to me that riders are usually so unforgiving of themselves for feeling apprehensive or frightened. *"I've been doing this* (cantered or gone out on the trails or led a horse from the paddock or jumped an in-and-out) *for years. One bad experience and I'm acting like a baby. I can't believe it!"* they declare in my office and in seminars. The majority of the letters I receive from riders around the world also say these things: *"I fell off*

*during a lesson and haven't been able to get my confidence back yet. I'm
worried I'm letting my trainer down."* And *"I feel so ashamed, I haven't gotten
on my horse since he bolted that one time."* And *"It's been over a month . . .
shouldn't I be over this by now?"* Anguished and impatient, these riders
implore me to tell them how they can get over their fears—immediately.

Sometimes I can do this; many times I can't—or won't. Fear is not a
random emotional experience. It has purpose: it signals that something is amiss. It has value: it tells you when you are outside your zone
of comfort or safety. No wonder we can't wish it away. It even has
evolutionary value; eons ago, those cavemen who respected their fears
survived the best. Of course the dangers then were a little different
(rock avalanches, mountain lions, poisonous berries) from what we're
talking about in this chapter, but nonetheless, our minds are wired
pretty much the same way.

There are other reasons we can't wish away our fears and anxieties
about riding accidents. Human beings have a phenomenal facility for
memory, and we remember (vividly) the panic of being run away with,
we remember the pain of our injuries, we remember the boredom,
restlessness, and frustration of being laid up. Moreover, being creatures with forebrains, we humans attach meaning to incidents past and
future, putting them into a larger context. A fall isn't just a fall but a
month out of work, a month without income, a month with no one to
muck or feed or tend to the rest of the family.

The Dangers of Pretense

Some people like to say that fear and excitement are two prongs on a
fork, nearly interchangeable if you can somehow manage "just to
think of your fear as meaning that you are very excited." Can you do
this? I can't. If I'm feeling scared, there is no other way for me to see
things at that time. And I'm not convinced that that would be such a
great idea either—to fake myself out, that is. After all, feeling fearful
or nervous is often your best cue that you may be overwhelmed,
overfaced, or underprepared, and I've seen too many riders ignore
these cues in favor of pushing on and trying to blow through their
fear. Not a good idea.

Overriding your fears, for one thing, makes for potentially danger-ous situations. Once a rider is feeling afraid on horseback, the situation has changed. It doesn't matter whether the objective reality is that the rider is or was capable of doing that very same movement or jump or gait one day ago. If her feelings about it are different today, so will her riding be different.

Second, ignoring how you feel about something is no better an idea with riding than with any other area of living. It's dishonest to your-self—disrespectful, even—and hinders you from learning to develop and trust your judgments about situations that you face. It also leaves people feeling (eventually) very disconnected from themselves—that is, they become so lost in a web of self-deceit and denial about their true reactions that they have too little awareness of their real internal states. For those who try unsuccessfully to deceive themselves, the re-sult is usually a feeling of inadequacy, because they can't "turn off the negative and turn on the positive"—one of the most inappropriately and overly used sport psych ditties around. It's the same way some depressed people feel when those around them chirp, "Oh, cheer up, just don't think about it!" Or "C'mon, snap out of it!" Yeah, right, as if it was ever that easy in the first place.

There's something else, too, that I've seen a lot of riders do, which often ends up backfiring on them. It's like this: Somebody has some-thing go wrong—let's say he gets run away with or his horse slips in the mud and falls on top of him. (Understandably), he is frightened for a while until he decides to confine the danger to that one specific situation. So, the rider says, "Oh, well, I don't have to ever be afraid of being run away with again, because I'm just not going to ride that horse again." Or "I don't ever have to give a second thought to my horse slipping and falling, because I'm just never going to ride in muddy conditions ever again." And so he goes merrily along, thinking he's over that little trauma until the next horse sees five deer on the trail and decides to run to Katmandu, or he rides an outside course that hasn't seen rain in weeks and his horse's hind legs start doing the bossa nova when going around the first turn. Such a rider feels he's been jumped in a blind alley. His whole house of cards, built on the presumption that he could control outcome by excluding the pre-dominant variable of past trouble, comes tumbling down. It's an awful feeling. Riders who had such experiences tell me they thought they had it all together now, but end up feeling worse than ever, disheartened and discouraged both. It's sad, because they would have been much better off coming to terms with the fright they had initially experienced, with the fact that horses—all horses—are basically silly creatures and may run away, and that sometimes the ground will slip away beneath you. But the situation is not totally out of our hands. We can minimize our risks by being careful and knowledgeable about our animals and about conditions, and we can decide what calculated risks each of us is or is not comfortable with, and then go from there. There is no honest way to promise yourself that you will never be run away with again. There are ways, though, to get over having been run away with without having to make such a false promise to yourself.

There's one other thing, though, that I must mention before we go on to better options for dealing with your fears, and that is the worry many people have about disappointing their trainers or family members or even their horses. In the words of one relatively new rider who fell off her horse twice, breaking several bones in the process, and who is now terrified to ride,

> *Every day I try to do my best to pretend nothing is wrong . . . instead of concentrating on my circles and serpentines, I'm wondering how far the hospital is from the barn!*
>
> *Worst of all is this feeling of letting everyone down. My trainers have nothing but patience, but I can't seem to shake the feeling of failure! Now I leave my lessons disappointed and confused . . . How do I deal with this overwhelming feeling of defeat?"*

How do you deal with it? You deal with it by recognizing that you're doing the best you can, that you're fighting your body's natural instincts to steer you away from perceived danger (whether real or not), and that you don't owe anyone any degree of bravery beyond what you're comfortable with. You probably haven't really let anyone down—we are usually much harder on ourselves than others are on us—and if someone like a spouse or father or friend or trainer does express impatience or disappointment, the problem is definitely his or hers. Don't make it yours. These individuals will need to learn something more both about human nature and about empathy. There are better ways to encourage, support, and, yes, even push those who need a little help getting over the hump and returning to their previous levels of riding than by humiliating them. Derision never inspired anybody.

Don'ts for Dealing with Fear

Here are some things to avoid doing to yourself if you are struggling with feelings of apprehension or fear about what's happening in your riding. Don't worry—I won't leave you stranded. The "dos" come afterward.

- **Don't** *try to ignore what you are feeling. Pretending that something didn't happen, didn't affect you, or isn't different usually serves only to make the problem worse; the larger part of you always knows what's true and what's not. Few people are good at that sort of thing, and even fewer can make it work for them. Besides, as I mentioned, it's usually not a very safe idea anyway. And while you're at it, don't spend a lot of time wishing that you didn't feel the way you feel. You do, and so be it.*

- **Don't** *fall into the trap of believing that if you refrain from thinking or talking about what you feel, the feeling will go away. It won't.*

- **Don't** *start calling yourself names or any thing like that. You are not a baby, a chicken, crazy, or a "Sunday" rider. You are normal. Disdaining yourself for your reactions to things is no way to start getting rid of them. If you believe that you really are a baby, then you'll never believe yourself capable of getting over how you feel.*

- **Don't** *make the relationship between you and your fear an adversarial one. Reread the part in Chapter 2 about the destructive effect of creating adversarial relationships between your self and your anxiety to see how counterproductive it can be.*

- **Don't** *blame your horse. He is doing the best he can with what are, admittedly, rather artificial conditions of living.*

What to Do Instead

- Determine the limits of safety for yourself and ride within these as you work to master the problem. And never ride beyond your comfort zone, even if it is smaller than what someone (or even you) would define as objectively safe. If you know that you and your horse could safely jump a two-and-a-half-foot fence but you are nervous at that height for whatever reason, then wait to jump that height until you feel more comfortable.

- Allow yourself to say out loud or privately exactly what it is you feel *if* you feel like saying so. Saying "This scares the bejesus outta me!" can be really good medicine for the ailment. Learn to find ways to be comfortable with how you feel as a first step to alleviating it.

- Ask yourself where and how you have mastered other fearful or overwhelming situations and revive the same personal resources you used then. Were you once frightened of driving at high speeds? Flying? Jumping crossrails? Moving up from ponies? Walking the dog alone at night? Eating alone in restaurants? Speaking up for yourself to authority figures? How did you overcome the problem? Did you do it alone or with the support of a spouse, trainer, friend, grandfather? Did you approach it from a perspective that would work well for you now? What actions did you take that helped; that didn't? What made the problem worse? Can you avoid that this time around? "Mine" your personal history for experiences and attitudes and actions that have worked for you before. Ask yourself not if but *how* you will rise to the occasion this time. Then do it.

- Commit to a first step somewhere in your attempts to deal with the problem. Decide to talk to your trainer about it, or drop down a division or level until you feel better, or add a lesson a week to work through the problem, or go back to foundation work (lunge-line work to develop a greater sense of balance and control, riding without stirrups to deepen your seat, etc.).

- Give some thought to why you are uncomfortable with your riding or some aspect of your riding. For those who were spooked by a fall or definable event, this is not a difficult question. But sometimes the change in how you feel may have come upon you more gradually, insidiously, and without a reason that is easily pinpointed. All you know is that your confidence has been gradually eroded over time and you don't know why. Thinking it through may help you find out and cope with the problem.

- Consider creating a ritual (see Chapter Six) that will enable you to put the problem behind you. Such rituals as burying or burning something symbolic from a bad riding experience (a piece of broken tack from a runaway, the prize list from the show where the fall took place, the day from an appointment book of that disastrous lesson) are extremely powerful.

Opting to Forge Ahead Despite Anxiety and Fear: Making the Difficult Decision

There are occasions where a rider or his or her trainer contemplates pushing ahead despite anxieties. They may do this because either or both strongly believe that the rider is indulging an anxiety that is out of keeping with the reality of the situation. They may also do this because one or the other is convinced that only by directly facing and taking on the feared situation will the anxiety go away. Either of these situations can work out well or not so well. How can a rider decide when it is best to opt out of a challenging riding situation and when it is best to forge ahead? Here are some questions and criteria to help you make that decision:

- How well can you trust your own judgment in this situation? Do you feel at a loss to know what's best for you to do (in which case you may want to hold off doing anything until you have a more accurate reading on your personal assessment of things), or do you have an opinion that you believe is informed and sound?

- What do the different members of your "team" say? This team includes your gut reaction, your trainer, your spouse or partner or close friend (if they are "in the know" enough about the sport and your feelings to offer useful advice), and other supports.

- What is the cost-benefit ratio? What could be gained by forging ahead, versus what could be lost? A situation where the gain is a Pan American team medal and the risk is overfacing a young horse is different from one where the gain for the rider is getting around a course at a local show on a new green horse and the risk is disability or dismemberment!

- Is there a personality trend that interferes with your evaluating the situation accurately and appropriately? For instance, are you chronically overcautious, to the degree that you wind up regretting how few things you try in life? This may suggest that a good personal goal would be to expand your tolerance for new and (carefully chosen) risky events. On the other hand, if you (or others) have recognized a reckless or impulsive part in your personality that sometimes lands you in trouble, you may want to err on the side of less risk than more, in order to compensate for that.

- If you were to decide to go ahead with the anxiety-provoking riding situation, are there junctures where you would feel comfortable stopping and bowing out should you change your mind? For example, if you were nervous about taking the next step up to the three-foot jumping division, do you think that you would let yourself pull up after the first line if things didn't feel right? If so, then you may choose to proceed. However, if you think that you could never do something like that, that you would be too embarrassed to stop your own round, then perhaps you are better off waiting. There are other ways, too, for you to maintain control over the situation while proceeding. Do you think that you could get to the show, look at the course, and decide then and there to leave your horse on the trailer? Do you think that you could leave the decision whether to proceed until after you school? Will your trainer respect your decision? Are you willing to eat the entry fees and shipping expenses? If so, then go ahead and proceed on this step-by-step basis, deciding as you go along just how far you want to take it on that day.

- Is there a trust issue with regard to your trainer? It's hard to assess the situation and come up with a good plan if you don't feel that you can really trust the advice of your expert. That's a bigger problem than whether to try cantering that day or to practice jumping into water. Deal with that issue first; otherwise everything else is for naught.

The Case of Kyle

Kyle is an amateur hunt seat rider in his thirties who had been riding for only two years before he spent a summer overmounted and overfaced with an unschooled horse who was a bit on the hot side. Convinced by an overeager trainer that he was ready to jump two-and-a-half-foot courses in hunter shows, he suffered through a handful of miserable shows before cashing in his chips with that trainer and moving on to someone else.

This new trainer was good and patient and helped Kyle with the basics of riding more than had the other trainer. He also kept him a lot better mounted, although the horse that Kyle ended up riding regularly was somewhat on the green side, albeit an honest and well-intentioned soul. Soon it became time to think about showing again, and although the new trainer tried to be careful and thorough, he did leave a few gaps in his preparation that left Kyle a little unsure about his readiness for jumping show courses with Simon. But come spring, they tried some of the smaller jumping divisions. Things went well. Kyle started to feel more confident and more comfortable with his new partners, equine and human.

Kyle's goal for the summer became the successful (that is, relatively dignified, disaster-free) completion of a two-and–a-half-foot hunter course at a show. It was two years since that bad summer. There was an appropriate division at a local show coming up, and Kyle's trainer encouraged him to give it a try.

Kyle was nervous in the days preceding the show and wondered whether he was ready and whether this was the right show to finally put his demons to rest. It was a larger show than some of the other local shows, and it tended to have more sophisticated jumps and courses. I'll share with you the way he processed his thoughts.

How well did he trust his judgment of the situation?

Pretty well. Kyle felt that he had learned a lot about the sport and about himself in the intervening years, and that his judgment about things was fairly on target—certainly much more on target than it had been the last time he contemplated competing at this level and height. His judgment of the situation now was of tempered confidence.

What were the different members of his team saying?

Kyle's gut feeling was one of uneasiness, and he was concerned that doing this show was just a little premature. His trainer was more comfortable with his moving ahead, but did say that they could arrange to meet at the show and take it one step at a time. Fair enough; Kyle liked the idea. His wife, a rider herself, had some misgivings about the reliability of the horse and about Kyle's preparation for the horsemanship questions he would be asked in that jumping division (for example, navigating in-and-outs and bending lines). She would support him either way, but was leaning toward his waiting for an easier show. Kyle balanced all these opinions, and decided to proceed along the lines that the trainer suggested, that is, going to the show and evaluating things once he'd seen the course, the fences, and how his horse schooled.

What was the cost-benefit ratio?

In Kyle's situation, the potential costs far outweighed the potential benefits. He could achieve an important riding goal and a sense of mastery over the psychological trauma of the falls and loss of confidence from years ago. These were important, and would do a lot for Kyle's sense of well-being and enjoyment of riding. But there was a fairly good possibility of his having a problem of some kind, and the consequences of that could range from the mild to the significant. Taking this into account, Kyle began to think that maybe he should hold off for a few weeks, practice some more at home on the kinds of obstacles he would face at the show, and look for an even smaller show, where the courses would be simpler.

Was there a personality trend in Kyle that would interfere with his evaluating the situation appropriately?

Well, Kyle did have an impulsive side, and never was one to shy away from an athletic challenge. Also, he was an ex-rugby player, and felt the humiliation of begging off a game was far worse than any dangers, even physical ones, that could be met on the playing field. He "learned" as a teenager that when the coach sends you in, you go, period. So this part of him was saying, *"If you're going to call yourself an athlete, then you're going to get your rear in that ring and do it!"* And another part was saying something like, *"C'mon, already, you're no longer a battlebound mass of testosteroned muscle and sinew. Now, you have something called judgment—not to mention a wife and two kids. . . ."* And so Kyle tried to keep the more thoughtful perspective in the forefront, since he knew that a large part of him still had that other, more "rough and ready" way of tackling things.

Could and would he bow out of the competition if he felt he was in over his head or if things suddenly went awry?

Yes, Kyle could and he would. He and his trainer discussed this option expressly, and both agreed that he could go as far into the day as he felt comfortable with, and that at any point—tacking up, looking over the course, schooling, in the middle of his round—Kyle could change his mind and pull up. This was very comforting for Kyle, and was ultimately what made him decide to go. He felt it took all the pressure off having to second-guess how he was going to feel at the show grounds, how the fences and the course would appear to him, and how his horse was going to be that day. Knowing there was a safe, easy, and sanctioned "out" on show day, Kyle was free to proceed.

Was there a trust issue present with regard to his trainer?

There was no problem here. Kyle felt that his trainer would be able to evaluate the degree of difficulty of the courses for this horse-and-rider combination, and then would have the opportunity to watch them school to assess their readiness. Since the trainer was as comfortable as Kyle with the idea of pulling out, Kyle didn't have to worry about being pushed to try something he wasn't ready for or simply didn't want to try that day.

Kyle decided to go, with the idea of riding in the division he'd looked forward to competing in. He would plan to get to the show grounds early, look over the course, see how he felt up on his horse, how they schooled, and so on. His trainer, agreeable to this plan, made himself available to Kyle at various times during the morning. But ultimately, Kyle decided not to show. Because the course set up for the day looked a bit advanced for Kyle's experience level, he had the trainer school the horse. Things didn't go well; the horse was stiff and crooked to his fences, and not particularly responsive to aids. There was no other class offered that day that would suit Kyle, so he opted to sit this one out and cheer on his barn buddies. All he lost was the cost of vanning and braiding.

One month later there was another show, a little smaller, with less intimidating fences and course designing. Kyle had had a further month of preparation, and had been active in structuring his lessons with his trainer so that he would be practicing exactly the kinds of courses he could expect at the show. The day was a success, with Kyle triumphant about having met (quite decently, too) his goal, the horse having had a positive showing and jumping experience, and the trainer pleased.

Trainers and Riders Dealing with Riders' Fears from the Same Side of the Fence

- *My trainer keeps telling me I'm ready to move up, but I really don't feel ready yet. I'd like another few months at pretraining level first. But when I tell him that, he criticizes me, sometimes in front of others at the barn.*

- *Last month I developed this fear of jumping oxers because my horse got tangled up in one at a horse show. My trainer wants me to jump a lot of them at each lesson, but I get dry heaves at the thought of jumping anything that is made up of more than one rail. I don't know what to do—I'm too embarrassed to say anything. I used to jump oxers left and right without a second thought!*

- *There's this new horse that I've been looking at with my trainer—she thinks I should get him, she thinks he'll be real fancy—but he's actually a little too much horse for me. She thinks I shouldn't pass up this opportunity, though, so I'm tempted to buy him, but to tell you the truth he scares me at anything more than a walk. He's a little big for me, too, but my trainer says bigger is always better. I don't know; it just doesn't feel right.*

- *I'm getting more and more nervous about going cross country, but my trainer just tells me it's all in my head, says I should just try to think positively.*

These are the types of comments I hear from riders all the time. They're trying to find an honorable way out of feeling apprehensive or frightened, or are trying to find their way back to the feeling they may have had as recently as a month or week earlier. They want their trainers to help them, but the process breaks down. The rider and trainer wind up on different sides of the fence, each trying to solve the problem in his or her own way, and not combining resources and thoughts in a constructive direction. Note that nobody needs to be at fault for this to happen. Different communication styles, different ways of dealing with fear, different levels of tolerance for anxiety states, and so on can account for two people getting derailed in this kind of situation.

Here are some tips for riders and trainers to help them remain on the same side of the fence, and to help trainers be supportive of riders who have already become afraid:

1. The validity, depth, or intensity of a rider's fear is a non-negotiable issue. However it appears in the rider's mind is how it is. Trainer and rider must always start from where the rider is, from the rider's perspective, both for the sake of rapport and for making the most effective changes in training or lessons. It is by far the more respectful position to take vis à vis the rider, and I've long believed that interventions stemming from a position of respect always fare better than those that do not respect the inner experience of the person who is seeking change.

2. Forget about trying to use logic. It has little validity in the province of emotions.

3. Discussing the matter off the horse sometimes works better than talking about these things in the middle of a lesson or schooling ring. Pick a setting that's conducive to candor and creativity.

4. Be sensitive to concerns about disappointing each other. A rider may believe that she is letting her trainer down by feeling

afraid; she may think that the trainer has put too much work into the combo for this to happen, or that the trainer pinned a lot of hope on her. A trainer can likewise believe that she has let her rider down if that rider has become afraid; she may feel that it was her job to prevent that from having happened in the first place. I encourage the rider and trainer to talk about dealing with fears and anxieties, too, and not just to appease each other with false reassurances. Each should speak to the other about their expectations for themselves and for each other in that context.

5. Give some thought to what the "barn word" is on riders who become frightened. Many barns have unspoken credos about fear and bravery, so the tolerance levels for each varies considerably. It would be very hard to be comfortable with your fear-related anxiety in a barn where everyone is trying to be more brave than the next person. Alternatively, there are some barns where it's *de rigueur* to be a little nervous about what's coming up in the next lesson, and it would be hard to admit that you've begun to feel rather brave about things.

6. When it comes to the actual riding part, start within your comfort zone and gradually, *oh, so gradually,* stretch. Don't overface yourself in a desperate attempt to blow yourself through your fear. There are few people for whom this is successful, and it most often backfires. Be patient and kind to yourself and explain to your trainer your feelings about the matter if he or she has it in mind to storm through it all. We don't retrain our horses this way, so why should we treat ourselves less carefully?

7. Be open, as a team, to where you need encouragement and where you need a little push out of the ditch. Although the rider shouldn't be commanded to do something that feels over her head, sometimes a little "clucking" on the part of the trainer gets enough confidence back into the rider to enable her to attempt something she can feel good about after she's done it successfully.

8. Both parties should also be sensitive to life changes in the rider that may be contributing to the changed state of mind. For example, a new parent, a pregnant rider, or a person turning a

certain age with some echo about physical vulnerability tied to it, may have rational or justifiable reasons for changing her mind set.

Masked Fear

Not everybody is comfortable feeling afraid. Many people think it unacceptable to their trainer, or incongruent with their self-image, or inappropriate for their level of training or expertise, or just plain ridiculous. They believe that they can or should be able to conquer fear with logic. Others worry that if they admit it to themselves, they will be opening the door to its negative effect on their riding. Usually, however, that's already taken place, and giving open voice to fear or anxiety will more often do just the opposite: attenuate the feelings by disempowering them. Anything is made more powerful by having been made into a secret.

Some riders will do all kinds of mental gymnastics to avoid an awareness of their fear, or to prevent anyone else from detecting it. These are some of the things I've found that riders do to keep themselves and others from recognizing that they are wrestling with such feelings:

- Become overly (and falsely) confident.

- Allow themselves to be overfaced in their riding by a well-intentioned instructor who knows nothing about how that person is feeling.

- Display nervous habits and pet mannerisms that become very noticeable.

- Displace (subconsciously reroute) the fear into other arenas, like repetitive worries that "the truck is going to break down" or that their "girth is going to snap any day now," even though nothing has changed in the condition of these things. Sometimes people will simply have a vague worry that "something bad is going to happen," but don't connect it with their riding. One rider that I saw privately had developed a very disturbing and irrational fear of brake failure in her truck that wound up being a displaced fear of her horse running away with her. Once she recognized and dealt openly with the real fear, the irrational fear disappeared.

Fear Unmasked That Turns Out Not to Have Been Fear After All

Sometimes things aren't what they seem. And sometimes this is as much a surprise to the person herself as it is to anyone else. While it's always important to take fear seriously, it's not always best to take it at face value. What do I mean by that? I'll explain by way of a story from my practice.

Several years ago I was helping a family of a mom, dad, and their four children. The older kids were becoming unmanageable, Mom and Dad were arguing a lot, and everyone was generally pretty miserable. One of the kids, a teenaged girl, announced in one session that her problems would be solved if her parents bought her a double bed. This would "prove" that they really cared about her.

The girl sat back, satisfied with her pronouncement. The parents looked at me, quizzically. I suggested that they take their daughter's request seriously but not at face value, that is, let the daughter know that they heard her and that they did take her feelings into account. They were also to let her know they were willing to do something about how she felt but that they weren't convinced the solution was literally a double bed!

It's this way sometimes with fear—it is not always what it seems at face value, although it's always something to be taken seriously. How so in riding? Well, I've seen people subconsciously develop fears of riding or of some part of their riding as a way to leave the sport. They may have had enough but don't know how to exit, gracefully and without shame. Or riding may be causing financial, marital, or logistical problems in their life, but they can't deal with that, so they subconsciously become afraid and stop riding. I remember working with a little boy who had developed a fear of jumping as a way to stop his parents from arguing about the money the sport was going to cost them as he progressed. Others develop anxieties and fears because those allow them to leave their trainer or get rid of their horse or buy a second horse. You get the idea. Fear, like many other feelings, is sometimes pressed into double duty.

The next chapter describes a tool that can help riders reshape or change altogether how they feel inside, either right before they ride or as they are riding. It's called the riding resource room, and is very helpful for riders who are trying to get over frightening experiences or timidity. But it is hardly limited to that, and can be a real boon for those who want to pump themselves up or otherwise enhance good attitudes they have in stock. The chapter following that one discusses the relationship between rider and instructor or trainer. Since the nature of this relationship can be of enormous help to the scared or timid rider by supporting and encouraging progress, or can exacerbate the problem, it is relevant to any of you who felt this chapter addressed your thoughts or experiences.

Chapter Eight

The Riding Resource Room

IMAGINE A ROOM into which you could step and compose yourself just before you walk through the in-gate at the National Horse Show in New York. And I mean *right there*—some area off to the side of the in-gate that awaits your arrival and serves to bolster your confidence, soothe your nerves, charge you up, or whatever else you need at that moment. You walk in, hang out for a while, get to feeling just right, remount, and go into the ring. Sounds silly? It doesn't have to. That room can be right there, at the ready for you, in your head. Portable, personal, and powerful.

I call this room the riding resource room—an inspiring and safe harbor within your own mind, a place of visual or perhaps auditory substance, a place where you can go whenever you wish to change, embrace, or celebrate how you are feeling at the moment.

I came upon the idea of a riding resource room when I realized that right before an important lesson, training session, or horse show, I'd find myself "in my head" for a few moments before getting on, or before entering the warm-up area, or before going into the ring. What I'd do is review what a trainer had once said that really boosted my confidence, or try to recollect the way I had felt at another show when my riding seemed effortless and fluid, or reread a passage in a favorite book on riding that describes in exquisite detail what a horse feels like underneath you when he is truly forward and round and happy. Maybe I'd allow myself to "hear" my imagination speak to me, saying, *"Have at it, kiddo; the course is yours for the taking."* Or sing to me a favorite tune that gets me fired up. Being in my room was always less a tactical review of the job ahead (that had already been done) than it was an immersion in an inner experience that would leave me feeling perfectly mentally prepared for what was to follow.

Who Should Use a Riding Resource Room?

- Anyone who needs a handy mental tool that can help alter how he feels on the spot. It may be someone who gets nervous, insecure, or distracted at "inopportune" times when riding, or someone who wishes to enhance his feelings of confidence, enthusiasm, or inspiration.

- Anyone whose negative thoughts intrude into the positive mental set which she has worked very hard to establish.

- Anyone who could benefit from discovering a stronger sense of the positive influences in, and supports for, his riding.

Creating Your Own Riding Resource Room

Creating your own riding resource room is easy. There are no rights or wrongs about how to make it up, and everyone's room is going to look different from everyone else's. The key is to make your room meaningful to you; that will give it the power to affect you later on. In essence, the riding resource room is a fantasized place that affects your experience of yourself at that moment. It has visual, auditory, olfactory, and kinesthetic (body awareness in motion and space) dimensions and works in part by repeated associations to desired feelings and mental states, and in part by helping you leave behind undesirable states of mind. This means that it will be made up of your memories, your songs and images, your look, feel, and smell. It can be a quiet or lively place, public or private, indoors or out. Yes, outdoors—there's no reason that you can't take a chunk of beach, a chunk of forest, or desert or garden, and make that the setting for your room inside your head. It's your head.

Have a room without walls, one without a roof, one that's a porch. Include music or don't. Include incense or don't. Mix and match. If this seems too fanciful to you, remember that our dreams don't follow logic and yet we allow them to affect our mood, our thinking, our beliefs. So have incense at the beach, have music deep in the woods, have your long departed grandfather—the one who was always so proud of your riding—sitting on a bench in your resource room. Have him remind you once again how happy he is with your enjoyment of the sport and of horses. Or put a phone in your garden so that your trainer from years ago, who one time said to you, *"You know, you can really ride a horse,"* can say it again while you wait in the starting box to go cross country in your first major event.

Put a VCR in your riding resource room and "watch" the tape (real or imagined) of your last, terrific dressage test. People whom you haven't seen in years, or since childhood, can be in your room, too. You can have one room for all occasions, or different rooms, depending upon your psychological needs at the time. These needs can include being relaxed, regaining composure, getting stirred up, feeling bold and confident, accessing aggression, and becoming more patient, among innumerable others. Use your creativity and play; the varieties of design are endless.

Constructing Your Riding Resource Room

Mentally derived rooms become much more substantive when they have a material counterpart. Therefore, I strongly urge people to construct the room on paper first. This way it really develops a look, a feel—a permanence. And making it real on paper will make it more real in your mind's eye.

To begin, sit down with a large sheet of paper and a pen or pencil and draw a generous rectangle or square. Don't fill the whole sheet; you'll need space around the outside of the box, too. Now, reflect on anything and everything that has ever been a positive force in your riding and begin "furnishing" your room with words, drawings, or names that represent (or symbolize) those positive forces. For instance, an exhilarating and revelatory trail ride might end up symbolized in your room by the name of the creek you crossed. A horse show where your riding all came together may be symbolized by a sketch of its prize list in the corner of your room. Throw in a favorite piece of tack, if you like. One western rider I worked with put in her room a special raised-cantle saddle she hoped to buy, because it symbolized to her the depth of seat she lost while schooling a horse that had shaken up both her position and her confidence.

You can include, too, the name of the song you heard on the way home from that special overnight trail ride, or the image or name of an admired rider. Essentially, the room should be a grab bag of your most poignant, memorable, and inspiring moments as an equestrian. And these moments, symbolized through your words, pictures, or scribbles, can be arranged in your room in any sort of way—jumbled about, on "shelves," on items of furniture, in a corner. The box, by

now your room, just has to be a place that you can mentally "get to" whenever you want, and where you can experience or remember something that will put you in the right mind set for the occasion at hand.

Now and then a rider will say to me, "But I can't think of anything!

The inside of my box is empty." And then she may discover that she never allowed herself the pleasure of hearing and absorbing positive strokes received throughout her life, or that she's been deaf to them. We all know people like that, they dismiss your positive or supportive remarks, behave in an overly modest fashion, or challenge your obser vations about their improved riding. Some can never be comfortable accepting a compliment and carrying it in their memory banks; such a remark makes them feel genuinely uneasy. Others act as if nothing positive has ever been said about them or their riding. And, for yet others, there really is a scarcity of positive riding experiences in their lives. If that is the case, there may be a real problem of the rider having been constantly overfaced, overmounted, or overambitious. That, then, would need to be changed.

Protecting Your Room

As you think back over influences that have supported your riding, you'll encounter some that have undermined it, too. These influences may be worries about how much the sport is costing or about how much time it takes you away from your family. They may include a previous trainer whose critical style left a seemingly indelible mark on your confidence, or a horse whose chronic stopping left you with a habit of riding too defensively. Maybe one of your parents once asked if you were "still involved with those crazy horses" and it's been reverberating in your mind, every once in a while causing you to doubt your commitment to riding. Bad shows, bad hacks, bad horses, bad training, bad tests all can intrude into your thinking just at the wrong time—as you're about to begin your work-off for the Good Hands class, as you are about to go through the starters for your jump-off, as you are mounting up for your first hunt of the season. The idea here is to grant these negative thoughts the favor of acknowledgment but forbid them entry into your room. They do get sketched or written in, but *outside* your room's boundary. Once you've done that, go back and thicken the walls to your room just to underscore that *in is in* and *out is out.*

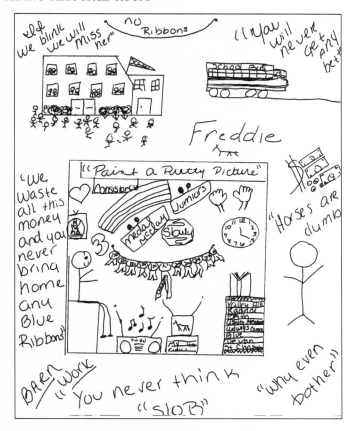

How It Works

A rider's construction of a resource room serves a number of purposes. For some, the process of constructing the room winds up being the most useful part, a thought-provoking and self-reflective experience more useful than the finished product. For others, the final space becomes an important part of their mental toolbox, and its power to alter how they feel at any moment grows stronger and stronger over time. What exactly does it do for riders? It does the four things outlined below:

1. First, the exercise helps a rider to cull a collection of mental supports and positive riding experiences. Most people have

one or two favorite riding memories and are amazed to discover, when doing this exercise, that there are bunches more of these stored away. They then become aware that they do have sources of encouragement, of inspiration, of solace, among other feelings, and that they come from their own history. This is the essence of resource retrieval: much of what a person needs to make desirable changes is already there inside. Athletes doing this exercise are also surprised to realize the power of songs, people, symbols, colors, and the like to effect mental change.

2. The second thing that the riding resource room does is offer a beginning model for segregating "bad" from "good" in the rider's mental set. The walls of a room represent symbolic boundaries between what's helpful to have inside one's head and what's destructive. The successful athletes who are consistent in their performances have developed ways of creating the ideal mind set and of keeping it from being disturbed by compromising thoughts, feelings, and memories. People don't need to remember the fall from their last lesson as they are warming up for the next one. They don't need to think about their harness pony having blown up at the far corner of the show ring just as they are about to round it. They don't need to feel tearful as they begin their equitation trip because they had a bad school right before. What the riding resource room can do is help riders make distinctions and drive protective wedges between what supports and what undermines, what comes along with you and what stays behind, what keeps you in the game and what knocks you out.

3. Composing a riding resource room can help you make an abstract problem into one that is more focused or better defined. Once you separate something from the muddle of thoughts and feelings surrounding it, it may become easier for you to figure out just what to do about it. For example, I had one western pleasure client who had experienced a fall that both seriously injured her physically and shook her up pretty badly psychologically. Surprising herself, she placed the horse outside her room. She hadn't realized until that moment just how

unsuitable a horse he was for her and how unattached she had, in fact, become from him. Seeing this horse on the other side of the wall from all those things that were positive influences and supports led to a decision to sell him and look for something that would be a more willing partner. Feedback later on indicated that that had been the right thing to do.

4. The fourth thing that this technique does is allow riders to walk around with their own toolbox of psychological resources. It is with them every time, all the time, which is very comforting, not to mention useful.

Ladies and Gentlemen, Choose Your Weapons!

Now it comes time to take this exercise a step further. You are going to select one or two mental weapons that you can use to deflect any negative thoughts or influences that try to intrude on you at unwanted times. A weapon can be the idea of steel-reinforced walls for the box containing your room, or a can of Raid kept in a corner of your mind's eye used to spray unwelcome thoughts such as *You'll never get through this lesson without hitting the ground at least one more time* or *Geez, my horse just doesn't have the brilliance of these others . . . we may as well go home.*

A mental fly swatter does nicely, too. Or a tennis player hired by you to "play the net of your mental field." When my mind set is right I often feel (rather than actually visualize) my room to be a clean clay court, protected simultaneously on all four sides by exactly that kind of hired gun, so to speak, one who slams away anything irrelevant or distracting to my thinking before it gets into my mental "airspace."

I've had riders choose to generate mentally a cadre of bruising bouncers at each window or door to their room. These guys serve to keep the "crashers" out—miserable thoughts or memories like that nasty judge who suggested you take up "another hobby." One client of mine, a hunt seat junior equitation rider, found that saying "Later!" to herself at the in-gate worked like a charm to banish homework worries, boyfriend worries, and competition jitters that tried to claim her attention right as she was about to enter the show ring. Computer buffs may find useful a "closed file" metaphor, where you take the unwelcome thought and store it away for the time being. Just click your mental "mouse" to achieve the desired result.

One of my favorite examples of a protective weapon is a drawing of Arnold Schwarzenegger as the Terminator, fearlessly protecting the sanctity of a nine-year-old boy's resource room.

Always keep in mind that these are abstract concepts—playful and transformable. Rather than looking for the logic and order in them, look for the magic and enchantment. These concepts—pulled together into rooms—become vehicles of inner transformation only if you work with them and make them yours. You must imbue the symbols and images with meaning so that your being in the room has a real impact on how you think and feel about yourself as a rider and athlete.

Using Your Room

When you move into a new apartment or house, it takes a while before it feels like home. So it is with your riding resource room. Its main purpose is to quickly and almost effortlessly alter the way you are feeling, in the same way your bedroom gives you a sense of privacy or peace the moment you walk into it, or the way that your office or desk encourages you to feel more workmanlike. This means that you have to build up that association between your room and the way you want it to make you feel, so you'll need to spend time in it, as you would in a new home—standing in this spot, sitting in that spot, and so on. Practice being in your room and generating the desired state or states. Do this at any time, at any place—for instance, while you're cleaning your tack, folding laundry, walking to lunch. You can do this while seated or lying down, but you don't have to; riders, like everyone else nowadays, have little extra space in their schedules for new projects, and I have found that they will generally try something new as long as it doesn't involve too much time. What you are looking for is that ideal mental set and the room so tightly associated that you feel yourself responding immediately when you step inside. As you work with this mental tool, you can expect it to function more and more efficiently and in increasingly challenging situations. Start playing with the concept during casual rides, or nonlesson situations, where you can dip in and out of your room and experiment with your mental and physiological responses. Can you capture the response within a few moments, or do you need a little more time to really have the feeling or attitude flesh out? Gradually work up to doing this in more mentally or physically demanding situations—a clinic, a show, a more advanced gait, a larger or more open arena, a different horse.

One other thing that enhances the effects of the riding resource room is for people to have a copy of their room somewhere on their person—in a pocket or purse, or easily accessible, such as in a glove compartment—where every once in a while they can pull it out and look at it, make it become real again, maybe add some new things. Some people like to leave a copy in their tack trunk, pasted on the underside of the lid, or inside their grooming box, or even inside their hunt cap.

Carl's Riding Resource Room

Carl began taking his first riding lessons to placate his horse-crazed daughter and has never looked back. He had just turned forty years old. He enjoyed not only spending time with his daughter around the barn but the challenge of mastering a new sport that so beautifully blended thoughtfulness, athleticism, and the art of negotiation. A physician, Carl approached his twice-weekly evening lessons with the same zeal with which he practiced medicine.

His problems with riding began after the instructor with whom he and his daughter had been taking lessons left the barn for another business opportunity. The two stayed put and settled in with the new instructor who came shortly afterward. This new instructor, Rob, had ambitions for Carl to show more frequently than the occasional local show he had enjoyed, and so accelerated his lesson plans. Before too long (and before he was ready), Carl was jumping two-foot-nine-inch courses on a leased horse he later discovered had a little habit of stopping. At Rob's behest, Carl began competing in the adult amateur hunter divisions at local horse shows, falling off no less than seven times in the first six weeks of showing.

One of the first things Carl and I talked about in his initial session was how he could regain control over his riding program by being more active in the decision-making process and by trusting and following his own judgment. I then had him begin to compose a riding resource room for the purpose of having him segregate the recent episodes of riding that were corroding his confidence and enjoyment of the sport from the earlier ones that had built them up. Though only three months had gone by since his first instructor had left, at this point Carl could hardly remember what it felt like to be comfortable and happy on the back of a horse. I hoped the riding resource room would help change that.

It was in the incarnation of the room that Carl once again felt the part of him that had been confident as a rider, that had been successful at horse shows (he had had two good showing experiences with the first instructor), and that had always looked forward to his next lesson. He put down in shorthand his memory of the two good shows, the names of riders he most liked watching on ESPN, and a few phrases he found really directed his riding in positive directions. Outside the room—well, you can read for yourself just how traumatic and destructive those three months had been.

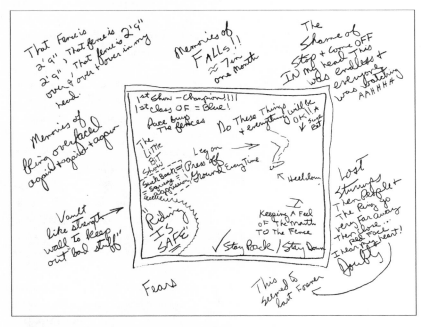

Carl did speak to his new instructor about revamping his riding program, and found him very responsive. The copy of the riding resource room that he carried around in his pocket affirmed Carl's recognition that there were things that worked for him in his riding and things that definitely did not. It also helped him ''seal off'' the negative experiences from the positive and more inspiring ones he wished to preserve. Although it took him several weeks to feel more associated again to the inside of the room than to the outside, he was

able to pick up where he left off seemingly so long ago. Carl loves
riding anew and, moreover, has learned from his experience how to
protect his enthusiasm in the future.

Paula's Riding Resource Room

Paula, a stock seat rider, sought help following the abrupt loss of
her prized penning horse, Winston. She had been champion with this
horse many times over at regional and national team penning events
and was well known and admired for her devil-may-care, no-holds-
barred riding. This horse and rider had over the years developed an
exceptional working partnership; each trusted the other. Paula was
devastated over Winston's death in a freak pasture accident.

Paula's new horse, Doc, had neither the training, experience, nor
heart of Winston. He also lacked Winston's manners and rideability:
Doc liked to rear, spin, and otherwise evade his work. After a year of
this nonsense, Paula had forgotten that she ever riproared through a
crowd of cattle or around a course of barrels.

I invited Paula to draw up her riding resource room during the first
of our three sessions. She put pencil to paper and came up with a box
filled with all the reminders of her better days. Winston is there, in the
upper right hand corner. In the upper left is a sketch of herself watching a video she had of a championship rodeo ride with Winston
several months before his death. Laughing, Paula added a bull whip,
too, "to get myself crackin' again!" The ribbons and trophies are
from her rides with Winston and the checked-off calendar represents
upcoming sport psychology sessions we had scheduled. The helmet
was representative of a concrete move she was going to make toward
enhancing safety factors—buying a special safety helmet—and the pic-
tured saddle was representative of an investment she planned to treat
herself to—a special raised cantle saddle that afforded a deeper and
more secure seat. What a wonderful mix of past, present, and future
resources Paula put into her room!

The creation of this room, coupled with a session of hypnosis, pro-
duced wonderful results. The thrust of the hypnotic work was to help
Paula reconnect to her earlier feelings of confidence, mastery, and
assertiveness while riding, and to underscore the fact that what she
once had was not lost to her but only rendered temporarily inaccessi-

ble by her more recent riding experiences. That the problem was an obstacle blocking the way to her "old" self (thus removable!), rather than the irrecoverable loss of her old self, was for Paula an enormous deliverance from anguish. This first session ended poignantly with both tears of relief and smiles of hope.

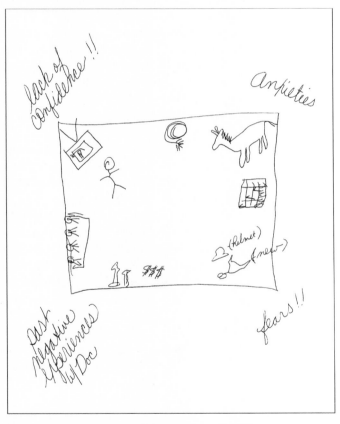

As soon as I saw Paula one month later, for her next appointment, I knew there had been changes; it was written all over her face. She'd started taking part in rodeos again and was feeling terrific. Her confidence was returning, and she had frequent and enduring episodes of feeling like her old self while riding and competing. When asked what she thought had made a difference for her, Paula cited the recognition that what she was seeking was something she'd once had and therefore could have again. A follow-up session two months later showed continued and sustained success.

Carl's and Paula's stories describe characteristic ways in which the riding resource room can be helpful. Other riders have used this tool to overcome fears of jumping or of riding bareback or of galloping across fields. Yet others have found it useful in reducing competition anxiety about horse trials or shows, in slowing down their "rushed" feeling of riding an equitation course or hunter round, or in overcoming a too-passive riding style. This particular instrument for transforming attitude and emotion is remarkably adaptable and is fun to fashion. It not only allows you, the rider-creator, to take an active part in a therapeutic change process, but also yields an immediate result in the form of a personalized sketch that can be carried around, stored away, revamped, pondered, or redone altogether.

We move on from here to the last chapter in this section of the book. Instead of describing a specific technique that riders can use to improve their performance, this chapter will discuss another important part of the pie that can have as much or more to do with how a rider is progressing and enjoying the sport—the relationship between riders and their trainers or instructors. It covers team building and communication skills, dealing constructively with differences of opinion or more frank conflict, and some of the external influences on riders and professionals that make for extra stress within the relationship itself. The chapter ends with several of the more frequent questions I am asked by riders about this topic.

Chapter Nine

Rider-Trainer Relationships

THE RELATIONSHIP between rider and instructor or trainer is not always simple and easygoing. Even though many people truly enjoy the social and working contact with the trainer, typically human issues such as authority and control, power and insecurity, as well as the need to feel in the right or understood or sympathized with or pushed or special can make the relationship between professional and student or client puzzling, sometimes frustrating, and even problematic. Alternatively, and sometimes simultaneously, many riders and trainers develop strong, mutually enriching, and enduring relationships. Riders will frequently credit their trainers with having been responsible for a considerable portion of their growth, not all of it riding-related. Trainers, too, will speak of their fondness for certain clients or of their appreciation of a client's support or commitment.

In general, all but the most distant or inconsequential of relationships need some degree of "caretaking" along the way to remain smooth. This doesn't always have to be a big deal. It doesn't necessarily require "talking everything out," or "sharing all your feelings and thoughts," or similar communication practices better reserved for our more intimate relationships. It can really refer just to keeping an eye on how a relationship is going, keeping a finger on the pulse of things. Examples of the questions you would regularly ask yourself are the following: *Am I comfortable talking with my trainer and working with him or her? Are there more and more things being left unspoken between the two of us? Are there things that either of us wishes the other understood better?* This kind of low-key, background monitering allows you to gauge the status of the connection between you and your trainer at any time. It also allows you to become more aware of the happenings in a relationship that please you. It would be nice to see more people (in all relation-ships) be more openly appreciative of those happenings. For instance, how often do you say to your trainer, or groom or secretary or busi-ness partner, for that matter, "You know, I've really been enjoying working with you"? Probably a lot fewer times than you've thought it (and if you haven't been thinking it much, you probably need a new trainer, groom, secretary, or business partner).

This sport in particular brings with it certain external pressures on the rider-trainer relationship. For one thing, equestrian sports have a competitive element and frequently draw people who are, by nature, very competitive. Two competitive personalities will always bump heads more often than two less competitive personalities. It is also a high-visibility sport and operates within its own insular world. Often the same people within a geographically large equestrian community compete in many of the same horse shows from week to week. Many of them know one another or have some sort of face recognition. They know who's buying a horse, who's selling, who just switched trainers, who changed barns. This means that everybody seems to know every-body's business. And since good results at the horse shows means good business for trainers, the pressures that trainers feel for their students and their own selves to do well in these very visible arenas can be quite intense. Some of these tensions may easily, and inadvertently, spill onto the relationships between trainer and rider.

Another factor complicating the relationship between rider and trainer is that there is a third party involved—the horse! This variable, unknowable to both people in exactly the same way, sometimes makes it hard for the rider and trainer to see things from the same perspec-tive. One has one understanding of the horse, while the other may have an entirely different view. If the trainer hops on for a moment to see what the horse feels like, it's already a different horse. Borrowing from physics, the Heisenberg Uncertainty Principle has taught us that once you become an observer of a situation, you have affected and thus changed it in some way. The horse that the rider was riding no longer exists; neither does the horse that the trainer was riding once he has returned it to the owner.

There's one other factor that sometimes complicates the relation-ship between rider and trainer, and this is that most adults loathe being beginners again! The majority of us feel that we have paid our

dues being beginners in grade school or in the early days of professional careers and the like. The idea of doing it again, of our own
volition, in our hobby or sport, is hard to swallow. Even if we are not
rank beginners, we're still junior to our instructors, in the role of
"learner" again, feeling awkward at times or—worse yet—incompetent. Sometimes, these feelings can affect the relationships we have
with our instructors, to the point where we end up bracing against the
very expertise we have hired them to demonstrate!

When the Road Gets a Little Rocky

Since many people don't give their attention to something until it's
become uncomfortable or become a problem, let's go ahead and talk
about the development of some tension or frank conflict in the rider-
trainer relationship.

No one likes discord, and few people are comfortable with interpersonal conflict, no matter how mild or appropriate or necessary. A lot
of people probably would like to be more comfortable, and more
adept, at handling the bumpier aspects of relationships, but aren't
sure how to go about doing that. And, as a result, many riders pretend
that everything is OK, or they figure that they'll just hang tough and
ride things out until the situation blows over. Many trainers do likewise, sometimes choosing to deal with a problematic situation by
labeling a student as one who "doesn't listen" or who "gives into his
fears too easily" or who "doesn't take her riding seriously enough" or
who "needs to 'get off her high horse.'" Yet there are many riders
and trainers who would very much like to resolve an impasse in a
friendly and compassionate way but simply don't know how to get the
process rolling.

A big reason for this is that many people are not comfortable bringing things up in the first place, even if the right opportunity presents
itself. I think the reasons are many:

- People rarely talk enough about their thoughts and reactions
  to things as they are happening in *any* setting—in their families, in their work relationships, even in their marriages. So
  much—too much—is left unsaid, glossed over, put aside.

- Many of the people who want to discuss matters more openly and more candidly don't know how to start. What do they say to open up the talk, they wonder? And when is the right time?

- Once burnt, twice shy: People who have had bad experiences when talking candidly with others in the past are nervous about doing it again. Who wouldn't be? Maybe a conversation was left with tension remaining between the people, or with people feeling more misunderstood or upset than when they started out. Folks can easily end up saying to themselves, "What's the use?" Or "I never should have brought anything up in the first place."

- Many people are not, by reason of their own culture or family upbringing, accustomed to talking about things in a way that truly reflects how they feel or think about a situation. They've been taught not to make waves, or to be mindful about saying something that might cause someone to be uncomfortable.

- Others worry that they won't be taken seriously, or that the other person will laugh them off, say they're "too analytical all the time" or "make things more complicated than they really are" or some other dismissive comment. I've heard trainers tell students that they are "thinking too much." When did thinking ever become such a bad thing?

- Sometimes it's just easier to hope that the problem will go away, and wait for that to happen (though it rarely does, of course).

Assuming Responsibility and Taking the Initiative

Everybody wants a mind reader. We want one for a husband, wife, mother, friend, business partner, therapist, professor, riding student, or riding instructor. When these people turn out not to be mind readers, we are disappointed, and sometimes we get angry. "You should know," we say under our breath, or, "You *should have* known." "You better know for next time!" we add for good measure. And this is spoken, of course, in the privacy of our own minds. Well, we could wait forever for others to guess that we have something we want them to know about in the first place and, second, to guess correctly what that something is. The self-righteousness that some people feel at "not being understood," when they don't make an effort to communicate what they want others to understand quickly becomes a hollow triumph.

It is always the responsibility of the person with something to say to make himself or herself heard. Given this, consider the following in your efforts to develop the best possible working relationship with your trainer:

✔ *Bring up your concerns early. Better yet, introduce them as a topic of discussion to your trainer before they get to the point of being a serious concern, for instance, while they are still just an idea or thought you have about something rather than a "problem."*

If you are worried that it is taking too long for your horse to get sold, ask your trainer his or her ideas for a next step. Should you put some more ads in the papers and horse journals? Should you lower the asking price? How does he or she typically handle the selling of a slow-moving horse? Don't grumble under your breath that nothing's happening.

If you feel that you're ready to do more advanced work in your lessons, bring the topic up with your trainer *before* you find yourself standing at the rail of horse shows, bitterly saying to your friend that you should be doing that level of test by now. Maybe your trainer was taking extra time because you had been overfaced in the past by another trainer and he wanted to make sure that that did not happen again. Maybe, as with my violist sister who plays professionally in a metropolitan city symphony orchestra, the trainer is so worried about you getting injured and its affecting your career that she becomes, at times, sweetly but unnecessarily overprotective. Or, maybe she was waiting for a cue from you that you felt ready to move on. Maybe she doesn't think you're ready for *xyz* reason, and has a different game plan in mind. You won't know unless you do something to find out.

✔ *Think through ahead of time exactly what it is that you want to communicate. Keep it simple, at least for openers, so that you stand*

*the best chance of having the other person understand precisely what
you mean. For example:*

"Listen, Rich, I want to talk with you soon about my lesson program. I've been feeling ready to move up a level, but
I don't get the sense that you necessarily think I'm
ready."

"Anne, I love your lessons but am sometimes left with not
enough feedback about what to do differently when I get in
trouble. Could you help me out by offering a couple of specific tips I can use when I'm schooling by myself and my horse
starts acting fresh again?"

"I don't want this to come out of left field, but is my mar-
ginal interest in going to shows boring for you come lesson
time? I'm aware you do mainly show riders. I just want to know
if your training me is still working out OK for you."

"I know you're trying to help me, Joan, but when you yell at
me in the schooling area of horse shows, I get really embarrassed and lose my concentration. Believe me, I'll be a much
more responsive student if we keep the instruction on a quieter level."

✔ *It's often helpful to add comments about what it's like for you to
bring something up, if doing so is difficult or anxiety-provoking.
Called "meta-comments," they speak to your experience of the moment and can go a long way toward making an awkward situation
less so. Examples of this include the following statements:*

"I feel a little nervous telling you this, because the last time
I brought it up with a trainer she felt challenged, and that's
not at all what I intend."

"I'm worried you'll think I'm a big chicken or not worth
training if I tell you how afraid i've become, but I don't see
any way around it. I hope you can understand."

"I know the last time we talked about this we both got a
little hot under the collar, but the issue keeps coming up.
What do you say we try it again?"

"I'm not sure which one of us feels more uncomfortable
talking about this, but I do believe we've reached a wall and
I'd really like us to figure out a way around it."

✔ *Try to describe to your trainer exactly what it is you want to do differently. Offer examples so that you present yourself as an active part of the change process, not just a complainer. Offer a specific vision of what you want.*

Tell your trainer what you need more or less of and at what times (more support by the in-gate, more constructive criticism during lessons, a more candid appraisal of the suitability of your horse for you).

Tell your trainer, without blaming, what does *not* work so well for you. The most well-meaning trainers use strategies that work terrifically with some students and backfire with others. It may be that he or she had no recognizable sign from you that a particular way of communicating or teaching was not effective or, worse yet, was destructive.

I'll never forget watching my husband being given a lesson by one of his trainers early last summer. John has always been an active and inquisitive learner, and he does ask a handful of questions during his lessons. His questions are always respectful, relevant, specific, and well thought out. They neither challenge nor provoke. And what he gets from his trainers in return are informative answers. Both parties enjoy the process. So this one day I'm watching John and his trainer discuss an instruction and a woman standing next to me on the rail huffs and says, "Well *I* never get lessons like that! It must be because he's a man!" And I thought to myself what a shame that she could not see this as other than a gender issue. The woman was unable to recognize an adult who had developed a mature, reciprocal working relationship with a trainer that both extracted the best that trainer had to offer on his subject and a mutual respect. Gender, schmender. Her immature attitude, lack of introspection, and sense of entitlement told me *exactly* why she didn't get lessons like that.

✔ *Make sure that your expectations about your riding, your horse, or your trainer are realistic before you express your point of view.*

There is often a delicate balance between getting our needs met in an appropriate context and fashion and looking for too much from the wrong person or in the wrong context. Being assertive must always be balanced with an acceptance of people's limitations or flaws or of the limitations of the situation. Run your thoughts by a friend or family member whose judgment you trust or who is familiar with the particular situation you are trying to handle. Not every trainer is going to be able to meet all our riding, training, and interpersonal needs, no matter how good or talented or personable.

Let's say, for instance, that you require a lot of support and contact with your trainer the day of the show and that your trainer has a number of students there besides you, plus other business to conduct. That part of you feeling left too much to your own devices, or abandoned even, may feel angry toward your trainer and push you to complain. The truth, though, may be that your trainer simply can't be everywhere at once, no matter how much you feel you need him or her. Another truth may be that you have become too dependent upon your trainer's presence and need to learn to become more independent when working your horse at a show. Another option is getting other people to hang with you throughout the day for support (spouse, barn buddy, or friend).

✔ *Along these same lines of personal reflection, try to consider what your contribution is to any rough situation that has developed between you and your trainer and figure out what you can do differently to alleviate some of the discord.*

Reflecting on your own self as a possible source of the problem is never easy. It's often humbling, too. People hate to be wrong. But it is important to do, both as a gesture of commitment to the relationship and as a way potentially of resolving the impasse or tension. If you've been under a lot of work pressure and have become a crank during your lessons, say so and apologize. If people at work have mentioned that you become patronizing at times, consider whether you've been patronizing around the barn. Maybe you've been too demanding. Maybe you've been too defensive. Maybe you've been too closed-minded about things. Just give it all a second thought and consider what you can do differently to make a difference.

✔ *Try also to show an awareness of the difficulties inherent in any trainer's job. Being sensitive to his or her occupational struggles and openly appreciative of where he or she has in fact been helpful can go a long way to enhance relations and to smooth over difficult times.*

If you see your trainer at the barn late night after night, say something about how time-consuming her responsibilities must be and that you appreciate how well she cares for the animals. If your trainer seems exasperated toward the end of a long lesson day, offer to bring in some coffee or sandwiches. Let your trainer know by saying so directly that you appreciate him staying late at the show to help you in that last class. If you're thinking it and it's nice, go ahead and say it. It's such a simple thing, but it makes people feel so good to be appreciated.

When Things Can't Work Out: Leaving Your Trainer

I'm big on people working things out rather than bugging out of relationships, be they friendships, marriages, or coach-athlete contracts. But sometimes things don't work out, or can't work out, or even after they do work out there is so much bitter residue that the relationship just doesn't feel right again. Then one or both parties may decide that it's time to make a change.

Leaving one's riding instructor or trainer is harder than most people realize. The recognition of this emotional difficulty usually comes just when it's time to make the break. (Parting with a trainer may be especially hard for kids.) Many threads of attachment go into the relationships between rider and trainer—they've spent months or years sweating, freezing, traveling, learning, talking, disagreeing, debating, worrying, celebrating together in the spirit of common goals. Add to that the trauma of leaving the facility itself, barn mates, and so on.

I don't have answers for making it any easier, but I can try to help riders in this situation appreciate why it is so difficult. Apart from the personal factors involved, major changes of any kind are hard on most people. People like to feel settled in with what's familiar, and will often opt to continue with the familiar way past the point where it's beneficial rather than moving on to something new. A lot of that is human nature, although some people are more or less comfortable than others with taking new steps.

In any event, if it seems as though you and your trainer have reached an endpoint, or your work together has become one of diminishing returns, it may be time to consider a different trainer. I always prefer to see a rider discuss the decision with the trainers rather than just announce plans to leave; this allows room for the trainer to suggest an alternative idea that may not have been considered yet, such as working for a while with a senior assistant, or taking several clinics with other trainers before making the final leap. It goes without saying that leaving on good terms feels a lot better to everyone than leaving on rank ones; after all, you'll probably wind up seeing each other at a show or the local tack shop sooner or later. And in the absence of good relations, cordiality is better than nothing—at least be civilized about the whole thing. And don't burn bridges with snide or aggressive parting comments. You just never, ever know where either of you is going to be two years down the pike. Besides, it's undignified.

Frequent Questions from Riders About Their Trainers

Private clients and clinic attendees often ask questions about how best to handle a particular situation that has come up with their trainer. Thinking they are alone in their dilemma, they're enormously relieved to discover that many others before them have asked a similar question and have experienced a similar dilemma. Here are some of the most commonly presented problematic scenarios between riders and their trainers. Answers follow.

My trainer has loftier goals for my riding than I do. How do I tell her that her ideas don't mesh with mine without offending her or making her angry?

Goal-setting should always be a mutual process between rider and trainer. No team, no steam. Having dissimilar agendas and expectations can easily lead to a host of different problems in both the training program and training relationship. Pull your trainer aside when things are quiet around the barn and explain to her in a calm and straightforward manner that you want to plan another program together. Tell her why you feel that her ideas about what you should be doing won't work for you, or don't interest you, at least for now. Then offer your goals and see if she feels she can work comfortably with you along those lines.

Help your trainer understand why the goals that you've selected meet your desires or needs better by understanding this process well yourself. Sometimes, the reasons we do or prefer certain things over others are not obvious. For instance, a trainer could easily think that you don't want to do more than a few local horse shows each year because of the added expense or time commitment. You may be thinking this, too, and then you discover that the real reason is your discomfort at being away from home overnight, or being far away from your family even for the day. The more honest you can be with others, the better they are able to support you in your choices in life. If you are frightened of the higher fences in the next division up, say so. If you prefer doing well in smaller shows to gaining more experience in larger, more challenging shows, say so. If you don't want to step up your goals because it would mean leaving behind your more limited horse, who you love, say so.

And, as far as the last part of your question goes, you can't always keep someone from feeling offended, or angry for that matter. One person is going to be better than some and worse than others at accepting differences of opinion without taking it personally or feeling criticized. As long as you bring issues, such as the one you mentioned, up in a timely, collaborative, nondefensive, and pleasant manner, it becomes the responsibility of the other to respond in kind.

I'm twelve years old and just got my own horse. I ride every day and plan on getting good enough to ride in the Olympics. I'm very serious about this, but when I tell my instructor she just smiles at me and tells me, "We'll see . . . ." My parents don't even smile—they just look at

each other and roll their eyes. How can I get my instructor to take my riding more seriously?

The best way for you to get others to take your riding seriously is for you to take it as seriously as you can. This means not only riding every day but trying to find as many horses as you possibly can to ride every day. Don't be picky or complain about the horses you get—ride anything that has four legs and a head (except for dangerous or very, very green ones). Remember, people are usually doing you a favor by giving you rides, no matter how old, ugly, poky, or unfit the horse seems. Taking your riding and your goals seriously also means learning everything you can about horsemanship, and about good horse and barn management. This means quietly following your trainer around (if she doesn't mind) as she oversees barn duties to observe how tasks, customers, horses, and employees are managed. It means working or volunteering your time at the barn in order to learn how to do all the things involved in keeping horses and horse owners or riders happy. Watch other instructors at horse shows, trials, club rallies, and the like to see how they might do things differently. Work out a summer internship with an equine veterinarian or chiropractor or massage therapist to see up close how they work and how they contribute to the overall health and well-being of performance horses. And, of course, take as many lessons and clinics with as many different instructors as you can afford.

Arrange to be a working student or trade services for lessons you can't afford. *Listen* to what they say, even if you disagree—be a sponge. You'll figure out later which learnings you want to keep and which you don't. Stand by the schooling area of every show you can get to, whether or not you are competing. Watch and listen to the professionals work with their students, work with their horses. Watch how the better students learn. Watch how they adjust their riding to the instructor's direction. Read. Rent videos. Read some more. Actions always speak louder than words, and never is this more true than when somebody announces the desire to reach a high goal. If you want to go to the Olympics, stop worrying about whether you are being taken seriously by other people, and begin your own program. Almost anybody will start to pay attention to—and take seriously—the person who means what he says and shows it through what he does.

Why do I feel so funny around my trainer? It's not really that I'm nervous, but I sometimes can't make normal conversation. I get kind of tongue-tied, and then at other times I end up running off at the mouth about anything. I really like her, and think she's a great rider. I like being around her at the barn and at shows, but I don't want to become a pest. Sometimes I find myself wishing I were her favorite student or best rider . . .

This question could come from the mouth of a child, a teenager, or an adult. The words may change a little, but the feelings and the puzzlement are pretty much the same. It is not uncommon for kids and adults to have this kind of reaction around someone whom they look up to, or with whom they work closely over a long period of time, or who is involved in an important aspect of their lives. This is a natural reaction, and while it may make us feel foolish or immature, it's really nothing to be embarrassed about. The problem is that it sometimes makes us feel a little self-conscious around these people or causes us to try to impress them. Trainers whom I've spoken to about this are often surprised to discover that adults feel this way. But many do. For most, the feelings go away over time. And if they don't, the worst of it for the younger people is that sense of not knowing what to say, while for adults it's usually having once again to deal with that awful feeling of self-consciousness that everyone thought they had left behind in adolescence.

My trainer doesn't believe I am as nervous as I am. She tells me to ignore it, that I'm chicken, that I should give up riding until I get over it . . .

This scenario is one of the most common that people present to me. And the trainer isn't the only one who doesn't take a rider's fear seriously—riders do this to themselves all the time. They dismiss their fears as childish, mask the fears with strained bravado, or chide themselves for feeling as they do. These are terrible things to do to yourself, and they usually don't help the situation anyway.

As far as I'm concerned, a rider's fear is *real*—it's a nonnegotiable issue. What it feels like to her is what it is. Period. It doesn't matter whether her trainer, barn buddy, college professor, mother, or grandpa thinks she is overreacting, overprotective, or overindulgent.

Besides, once a rider feels a situation to be dangerous, it usually has become so, if for no reason other than the negative way in which her uncertainty affects her riding. Also, I generally tell people not to bother with efforts to try to talk people out of their fears; logic and rationality have little currency in the playing fields of emotion and anxiety.

So, now, the immediate objective becomes one of limiting your riding, for the time being, to a zone in which you feel comfortable and safe. While there are times when a rider needs a trainer to push her forward, here I'm just going to address those times when a conservative approach is more appropriate.

A good first step is to approach your trainer when neither of you is riding, and tell him or her that you need to talk about feeling frightened when you're on your horse. Talking while unmounted gives you more time to explain how you feel than you'd have during a lesson. Also, during lessons, it's too easy for your trainer to say, "Oh, go on now, just try it and you'll see, you'll be fine . . ."

When you finally do sit down with your trainer, take your time explaining that you really are becoming more and more uncomfortable riding your horse, and that you've tried to ignore it but that hasn't worked, and that you don't want to stop riding until you "get over it." Ask if he has some specific and concrete ideas for making you feel safer while riding (for example, riding only under his supervision, riding on a longe line, more work on basics, lowering the fences, using a smaller ring), or for settling your horse down, if he is too hot (for example, more turnout, less grain, getting him schooled more, different tack). Try to keep the conversation going until the two of you come up with at least two ideas you'll feel comfortable trying.

Incidentally, people are always very surprised at how much their anxiety lightens when they feel they're being heard and taken seriously by those who matter to them. In addition, being heard moves the recipient of that information to share responsibility for monitoring the anxiety level. That way, you, the rider, don't need to track your anxiety all by yourself, but can use your trainer's observations and experience to help you gauge how much you should be doing at any particular point in your training.

I feel very criticized by my instructor all the time, and I'm not enjoying my lessons anymore . . . My trainer compares me with his other students and makes me feel bad about my riding . . . I want to tell my trainer what I'm feeling, but I just can't talk to her . . .

When it comes time to answer these questions, it is apparent that they are far more alike than they are different from one another. They all speak to a need on the part of the rider to come forward and speak candidly with the trainer about what's become bothersome. There are few other options except for suffering in silence, waiting (forever) for the trainer to somehow "figure out" what the problem is and spontaneously change, leaving the trainer, or leaving the sport. None of these choices has much appeal for most people. Consider the point you want to make, think ahead about how to present it, pick a good time to approach your trainer to talk, keep your points simple, believe in your privilege to be listened to and have your perspective taken seriously, listen in turn to your trainer's perspective on the matter, and be active in suggesting solutions. It's your sport—do what you need to in order to protect your enjoyment of it. Relationships—professional or otherwise—often need some help and reshaping to keep all parties satisfied over the long haul.

These questions and answers conclude this chapter on rider-trainer relationships, which wraps up this section of the book written specifically for the rider. But don't stop here. The next section, written for the equestrian professional, has much to offer the nonprofessional rider, even if it's just to view things from a different perspective. The first chapter in this next section deals with the way in which psychology influences teaching and learning, while the second deals with the variety of business aspects involved in managing an equestrian operation, including such things as professional-client relationships. The final chapter in the section covers work stress and the professional, offering ideas for dealing successfully with the myriad of stressors that come a professional's way and creating positive working and learning environments.

Part Two
For Trainers and Instructors

Chapter Ten

The Psychology of Teaching Sport

ANY TEACHER worth her salt knows that there's a whole lot more to instructing than telling people what they should know. Besides the curriculum itself—whether history lessons or calculus, business or riding—teachers know that there are ways to influence the rate at which their students learn, as well as how much material actually gets retained. There are also any number of ways to help students become open to different ways of doing something, or to change old habits that don't work well.

This chapter covers the different psychological factors that influence teaching and learning. We'll also review the many relationship issues that affect the "space between" two people, where lots of learning typically gets lost. A riding instructor who says that it's up to riders to get what they can from what she has to offer is like a psychotherapist who describes herself as a "dispenser of mental health," without regard for what she needs to do to make the learning or change process inviting and meaningful to clients. A similar analogy could be made to a schoolteacher who feels that her responsibility ends with the simple imparting of information. The teaching and learning process is an interactive one, and, because of that, can never be studied solely from one side (teacher) or the other (student). The quality of the relationship between teacher and student plays a major role in the outcome of this process and so deserves at least as much attention as we'd pay to such pieces of the pie as lesson planning or memory.

It's the Same Ol', Same Ol' . . .

Most riding instructors rise to their positions without benefit of any kind of formal training. And so they teach the way most of us parent: believing that for the most part what we got was good enough for us, we figure that it will be good enough for the next generation, whether of children or of riding students. Not enough people (parents or instructors) think about what they could do to improve on earlier models. And so things continue as before, flaws, gaps, and all.

But, at the risk of migrating from the ways of our elders, mentors, and caretakers, we need to move beyond what we learned was the "way things are done." For one thing, the applied sciences of teaching, learning, memory, and developmental psychology are always discovering new things. And for another, complacency and self-satisfaction can be dangerous; there is always more to learn. Moreover, certain traditions are worthy of being carried on, and some are not; those of us in the position to pass along a body of knowledge need to be active in deciding what to hang onto and what to let go of. This way, teaching stays fresh and current and relevant.

Some More Hidden Obstacles to Learning and Progressing . . .

To the casual observer, teaching riding looks pretty simple: you tell people what you think they should be doing on top of their horses. Do this; do that; do more of this; don't do so much of that. People who don't understand how therapy works think the same of it—that it's easy, a simple process of giving out information and advice. But tons of obstacles can prevent instruction from being acted upon, whether we're talking about therapy or riding. Some of these obstacles are the normal and expected hurdles of any training process, while others relate to emotional issues that either a trainer or rider (or both) is wrestling with. Often enough, these folks may not even be particularly aware that a psychological bugaboo is holding them back or interfering with their efforts to teach or ride or relate better. That's when frustration can build and spill out into many different aspects of the person's riding or business, or even family life. Here are some of the obstacles that instructors and riders have faced in the teaching and learning process that have come to my attention:

- overfacing or being overfaced;
- lack of faith in a rider's, or one's own, ability to change; a sense of hopelessness about oneself as capable of doing better;
- trainers' subconscious inability to let riders progress past their own level of riding (i.e., a trainer nervous about jumping three feet six inches has riders all doing the three foot division or below even though they are ready to move up);
- trainer assuming that a rider has become too dependent when the rider is really lost in the training process;
- rider's anxieties or fears about becoming too good or even better than trainer;
- power and control battles that don't allow for open communication, or that prevent the rider from "taking anything in" from trainer;
- poor fit between trainer and rider (personality, business style, availability, goals, intensity or dedication level, teaching style);
- inadequate support or too much hand-holding on the trainer's part;
- passive learning style on the rider's part.

Many of these scenarios are addressed later in the chapter. Some are natural byproducts or phases of the teaching-learning process and, as such, are best dealt with by understanding and acceptance rather than by denial of their presence. And since an ounce of prevention is worth a pound of cure, I'll also talk about what trainers and riders can do to obviate such situations altogether and enhance the processes of teaching and learning riding altogether.

You May Not Sew, but You Still Gotta Learn How to Tailor

Sensory System Preferences

The topic of different sensory system preferences was introduced in Chapter Four on mental rehearsal. Since people experience certain activities in the world in slightly different ways—for example, predominantly through their visual senses, or auditory, or kinesthetic (sensitivity to movement and balance within one's own body)—it only makes sense that they will prefer certain modes of learning about the things that go on in the world as well.

I personally like exploring my environment through sight and touch. In school, I always loved taking down notes, looking them over later, highlighting them, even feeling the indentations of different pen markings on the paper. Lessons taught with pictures and graphs were good, and those taught mainly through lecture were not; I'd get distracted, bored, drift off. I learned best when learning involved the visual absorption of something.

My husband, John, is the auditory guy. He sits in the same professional presentation as I do at a conference and remembers nearly everything the presenter said, while I've spent the hour practicing leg yields in my head. Put on a visual demonstration of some therapy idea or intervention, however, and I'll soak it up.

As a riding instructor, you can enhance your students' responsiveness to instruction by channeling some of it toward their preferred sensory system. To do this, consider which of your students learn about correct movement and pace best by watching a horse go correctly before being expected to execute it themselves. Which learn best by simply doing it in a trial-and-error fashion, and which by hearing you describe the specific sequence of movements and application of aids in exacting detail? For whom does it change when they get nervous? Keep in mind that you don't need to be the one figuring this all out for each of your riders; let them answer these questions, too. It's important for them to be an active part of the process. Most adults have some awareness of sensory system preferences anyway, and kids and adults alike can enjoy learning about how they best learn.

How does this translate into instruction? Well, contrast the following two directives, the first spoken for the rider strongest in her visual senses: "Jackie, look down and *see* where your leg is positioned in relation to your hip—that's just what you want."

To the second, more of a "feel" rider, you'd say, "Noah, can you *feel* the angle of your hip and the position of your knees? Take a moment to feel how they are more open now—that's what you want!"

To riders who are learning about horses' rhythm, you might say to the auditory person, "Can you *hear* the rhythm in the flapping of your bell boots?"

To the kinesthetic person (the "feeler") you'd say, "Just focus on feeling the rhythm of the trot. You can even close your eyes for a few moments to really get an internal sensation of it."

Remember that not everything you say to your riders needs to be as tailored as these examples. You've got to be practical, and it would be impossible to customize every detail of every lesson. But even saving this technique for a few select or especially important instructions or concepts per student might make a huge difference in their rate of absorption.

Last year, when I was giving a talk to a group of riding instructors, one of the attendees asked me how this concept applied to group lessons. She thought that things could get pretty crazy if she tried to tailor instruction for more than one person at a time. And she was right. What you need to do is pick and choose the times, and the lessons, where you think it would work. Where you think tailoring instruction to sensory system preferences would get too complicated, or where you think you would feel too distracted by considering each person's learning needs in a group lesson, save this kind of instruction for more private moments. In fact, your student doesn't even have to be mounted to benefit from your insights about this. You can always encourage someone to go back over his lesson at the end of the day and get a mental feel for that good forward trot rhythm he was able to get out of his horse. The idea of using sensory system preferences in teaching riding is not about revamping teaching styles but about having the option to tailor in this way whenever you think it would help a rider better grasp what it is you're trying to teach.

The "Benevolent Rider"

In the mental health professions, the concept of the benevolent client refers to a therapist trusting that the client is well intentioned, no matter how irrational, counterproductive or self-destructive he or she appears. The therapist trusts that the client acts that way not because he or she is mean, manipulative, or flaky but because somewhere in that person these actions have a "logic" to them. They make sense. And not even the client himself or herself may understand what that logic is at a particular moment. Let me give you an example.

A young teenager with no history of school problems suddenly is getting into a lot of trouble in school. This results in many teacher-parent meetings, which end up reuniting, at least for these meetings, his separating parents. Manipulative? No. It's not even conscious on the boy's part. He's not aware of why he's getting into so many arguments with his teachers and peers—he just is. But some part of him deep inside desperately wishes his parents to be together again, even at the expense of his schooling, so a part of him starts provoking arguments with others and being "difficult."

Here's another example of how we can wind up doing something that seems irrational at first glance. A woman who is frightened of intimacy in relationships suddenly, and unwittingly, acts in ways that push away her new boyfriend, of whom she is very fond. Neither understands why they are arguing all the time. They are both saddened and frustrated, and speak of breaking the whole thing off. Crazy? Only to the casual observer. The truth is that sometimes our fears and anxieties rather than our common sense rule the day, and the worst part is that we often don't even recognize when it's happening. A husband subconsciously directs his back pain to become chronic because he's learned that when he and his wife are worried about his health, they don't argue as much. A junior in college drops out of school for no apparent reason and returns home, protecting his mother from her loneliness and guilt over her recently departed husband. This stuff happens all the time.

In my practice, I often think of people's problems or symptoms as "communications" of sorts. To me, the boy acting up in school is saying, in the only way he knows how, "Mom and Dad, I'm scared of losing you and our family. Please stay together!" And the woman who pushes her boyfriend away is saying, through her actions, "I really like you a lot, so much that it scares the willies out of me, so I think I'll just bug out of this whole thing altogether and avoid the anxiety of getting close."

The therapist helping the boy through his difficult period would do well to assume benevolence on the boy's part, to assume that he is really trying to preserve the only family he's ever known; it's just that his method is a bad one and desperately needs changing. And the therapist helping the woman who is pushing away perhaps the most suitable partner she's ever known would do well to assume benevolence on her part, to assume that, rather than being ridiculous or "too picky," she's reacting to an anxiety about intimacy that is so powerful that it overrides her wish to find a man to settle down with. The therapy, then, revolves around simultaneously maintaining compassion for the person's plight and urging her toward finding better solutions.

These ideas are quite relevant to the teaching professions, including riding. Riders get stuck in bad habits, slumps, ruts, or negative patterns of responding to their horses, not necessarily because they're stubborn, thoughtless, lazy, untalented, or not otherwise trying hard enough, but because of some inner obstacle that prevents them from easily making the required change. This is where the benevolent rider idea is useful; in trusting that these obstacles have some "logic" to them that's not obvious, but, when understood, can more easily be dealt with. The obstacles could be anything, but the following are what I've discovered to be some of the more common blocks to absorbing or retaining instruction, even at its best:

- Despite all the apparent mental logic, the body believes that what the rider is doing is exactly what he or she should be doing. As an example, consider that natural kinesthetics and instinct dictate that when a person feels in danger of falling off a moving animal ten times his or her weight, his shoulders and other hard parts of the body hunch over to protect the innards. Nature is very smart, and she doesn't like to defer to athletic direction.

- A rider can get so anxious about doing the right thing that she becomes utterly paralyzed for fear of doing it—or anything, for that matter—wrong.

- Some people have so little faith in their ability to change that it's hard for them to take active steps in that direction. They get stuck in a self-image and self-identity that project hopelessness and rigidity. These then become a self-fulfilled prophecy.

- Some riders become so nervous about disappointing a well-liked, well-respected trainer that their nervousness interferes with their ability to focus on what they are doing and maintain any changes made. The change process involves not only the moment when the person fixes the problem, but the means by which a person maintains the change. Such a rider ends up responding well to direction but not in reinstructing himself, because the anxiety is too distracting. Since developing new habits involves repetition, the changes never solidify into a habit.

- Change is easier when people have reference experiences to draw on. When a rider does not know what he is looking to have happen, he can wind up spending a lot of time—weeks, months, a year—floundering around up there searching for a desirable feel or experience. Since it still seems foreign, he never knows when he has it right.

Tension often arises between trainer and rider when the rider feels that the trainer isn't appreciating how hard the rider is trying to do what's being asked. At the same time, trainers often feel that their riders aren't listening to what they're saying, or aren't trying hard enough. Assuming benevolence simply means that you see the rider as doing her part as best she is able at the time. There will, of course, be times when that's not true and another problem is at hand; part of an instructor's wisdom is distinguishing between the two very different situations. What does this benevolent rider idea look like in action? What does an instructor actually say? The following are some examples:

- Hey, Katie, we've been working on leg position for weeks now, but not much seems to be happening in that department. I remember last summer when we worked on your hands, and the changes came pretty quickly for you. Why do you think this seems so much harder?

- Mark, what do we need to do differently here? I don't think what I'm telling you is working.

- Judy, you look so frozen up there, as if you're afraid to move! I'd rather have you try something that doesn't work than do nothing. I never mind mistakes or bad decisions that you come by honestly.

- Remember that lesson last month where you forgot about getting the right spot and just rode around the course? And every fence just came to you nice and neat? Forget the fences, Maggie, and just try to recapture that rhythm you had. In fact, I want eight ugly fences!

- Sarah, you talk about yourself as if you're not capable of change. Does it really feel like that to you? What do you need to feel better about your ability to learn this sport?

When Change Doesn't Happen as Quickly as You Want It to in Your Rider . . .

1. Ask yourself whether you're working harder than your student for the change. If so, something's amiss. She has got to be the motor behind things happening differently. Remember, missionaries often get killed; don't make improvements or changes your personal crusade.

2. Try it all again in a week or so, after having given it a rest. Like the centipede who is asked how he manages to coordinate one hundred limbs and then ends up falling, too much attention to something simple often entangles everybody.

3. Ditch the fantasy that you can control the degree to which your rider wants to improve. You can't. Surrender to the reality that, ultimately, it's her choice (and her prerogative) whether or

not to change something. Respect a student's right *not* to change, even if it means you then choose not to work with her.

4. Don't take it personally. It's always a good idea to consider what you, as trainer, can do differently to help your student over the impasse, but once you've done that, know you've done your job. If you start regularly taking a rider's progress or lack thereof as a personal reflection of your value or talent, you can wind up feeling overly committed to an event that's not yours to control in the first place.

The Power of Inspiration

The teaching trades have always considered criticism (constructive or otherwise) an important part of the learning process. After all, people learn by being corrected, right? Well, yes, but have teachers overlooked the power and advantages of using inspiration to help people grow? I think so. There's nothing so motivating as working with an instructor who thinks wonderful things about your riding, or at least about some parts of your riding.

I'm often struck by how many instructors adhere to the notion that if they compliment their riders a lot, these riders are going to get "big heads." I don't think it's ever the compliments themselves that are the problem; it's how those compliments are used, psychologically, by the students to whom they're directed. Some will use them appropriately to boost their confidence and feel good about what they're doing. That is healthy. Others, though, are going to use favorable words to get hot on themselves, to self-aggrandize, and sometimes as an excuse to stop learning. But even though there's the risk of this happening with your students, you don't want to throw out the baby with the bathwater. Be as liberal as you feel you can be with your compliments, and then, if the student is using them destructively, do something about that. For example, you may say to that student, *You know, Deb, I really like telling people when they got it right, but every time I do this with you you use it as an excuse not to listen to me for the next few lessons! Don't make me cheap with your compliments, kiddo! We all, you included, still have lots to learn.*

Some instructors tell me that students come to learn what they're doing wrong and not to hear about what they're doing right. I don't buy much into this any more than I do to the last idea. Teaching is more than telling people what they need to do differently. It's also affirming the efforts of others, confirming that what they think is working is, and supporting steps in the right direction. If you get too stuck on this idea of only speaking up about what's wrong, you may end up becoming an uninspiring, withholding instructor rather than the major transformational force you can be in your students' athletic lives.

Most often left unsaid are the trainer's spontaneous thoughts about a rider that reflect positive impressions, a "pleased sense" regarding some aspect of that student's riding. These thoughts may be about a rider's good decision-making skills, or talent for sitting quietly on a hot horse, or degree of dedication. Most trainers do say their fair shares of "very good" and "that was nice," but they don't say often enough other positive things they're thinking to themselves, such as, "She really does have a way with a hot horse," or "What a dead eye! She nails every distance and she's barely been doing this a year," or "She is one brave little girl; I think she'll go places."

In fact, research done on the influence of coaching behavior and children's psychological development has demonstrated that it is the *quality* of positive reinforcement that really makes a difference in a child's self-perception regarding skill level and motivation to achieve. One voice of wisdom in the equestrian industry, the renowned saddle seat equitation trainer Helen Crabtree, considers the building of a "desire for excellence" to be the moral obligation of instructors. As someone long interested in the psychology of mental health, I've become very aware of how an individual's pursuit of excellence grows out of robust self-esteem, a willingness to take risks, and an intense enjoyment of personal challenge. These things do not happen when a child's support system is devoid of meaningful, specific, and heartfelt reinforcement.

The Importance of "Because"

Years ago an interesting little experiment was run in a university library. A "fake" student walked up to a line of people waiting at the library's single copy machine and asked to cut in so that he could make his one copy. No one let him in. On another day, the same student again walked up to a line of people waiting at the copier and asked if he could cut in *because* . . . and then he gave a reason. Some reasons were sensible (the dean needs a copy of this contract right away), and some were irrelevant (it's Hannah's fortieth birthday tomorrow). Whenever he said the *because,* people let him in. It didn't matter how believable or inane the reason; the *because* regularly worked to elicit everyone's cooperation.

So tell your rider that you want him to keep his hands a little lower today, even though all month you've been working on carrying them up, *because* this horse's head carriage is different from his own. Tell your other rider that you want a more boxed-in frame for today's lesson *because* you want her horse to start stepping up behind and you think the horse is ready now to jump more comfortably off her hindquarters. Tell another that you want him to canter on more strongly, even though you've recently been working on slowing things down, *because* his horse has started to back off the bridle.

Working with Fear in the Rider

One of the most common questions asked of me by trainers is how best to handle the rider who has become afraid. Being afraid for one rider may mean not being able to lead her horse from the ground; for another it means jumping into or over water. There's no comparing when it comes to fear. Afraid is afraid is afraid, and one person's fear feels as nasty to him or her as anybody else's.

For starters, an important thing for both trainer and rider is to acknowledge and accept the fact that there *is* fear or anxiety or apprehension lurking rather than wishing or pretending it away. A trainer who is in cahoots with her rider about hiding from unwanted feelings robs both people of a lot of mental energy that could be otherwise available to resolve the problem causing the fear or anxiety. Here are some other ways to deal constructively with your riders' scared feelings:

1. Encourage your rider to discuss his fear with you. Don't join him in keeping it hidden; this only makes a bigger monster out of it. We human beings have never been good at banishing unwanted thoughts from our minds at will and on a moment's notice. In order to command yourself to *not* think of something, you need to think of that very thing before you think to not think it. The whole thing is an impossible mess. Talking about being afraid does not make things worse. Not talking about it *does*.

2. Avoid the temptation to take your rider's feelings or situation personally. When that happens, the trainer's personal investment in "getting the problem over with" can sometimes lead to well-meaning but misguided attempts to hurry a rider over her fear, attempts that often backfire. The other risk—no less serious—is the loss of rapport between trainer and rider as the rider feels her fear is not being taken seriously, as well as her potential loss of confidence in the trainer's judgment. A more useful approach is working alongside your rider, supportively, and helping her figure out and tell you what she needs in order to be more confident when riding.

3. Consider alternative training regimens as soon as you spot trouble, rather than doing more of what is not working. In certain cases, encouraging a rider to confront the feared situation *will* be the correct approach; experience and sound judgment are what make this kind of call a good one or a real dud. A useful rule of thumb is limiting the rider to her comfort zone of riding. If a rider was run away with at a canter and now is nervous to ask her horse for that gait, don't force the issue nor embarrass the rider by reminding her how many years she's been cantering. She's probably already feeling humiliated by her inability to do what she used to do. Hang with her

until she feels ready to try cantering again, or think together of other ideas that can help her move closer to her goal of cantering comfortably again; for example, cantering on a longe line or cantering on an old-timer school horse until cantering is no big deal. Don't try to blow through a rider's fears by forcing her to confront it if she doesn't want to. If you were scared of spiders, how would you feel about having to spend twenty minutes with a few dozen of those creepy crawlers?

4. If several of your riders are nervous about some aspect of their riding—even different aspects—encourage them to help one another instead of keeping it a secret. Don't betray confidences riders have shared with you regarding their fears, but see what you can do to foster an open and supportive barn atmosphere for riders who get scared. It happens to all of us at some time or another.

5. This next suggestion may be tougher to follow through with than the others. If a lot of your riders are becoming, or have become, fearful riders, or are backing off what had been the game plan, consider what you may be doing to contribute to the problem. There's less shame in recognizing a mistaken teaching philosophy or course of action than in forging ahead self-righteously and without reflection about your training method. Maybe what you do does work fabulously for ninety-nine out of a hundred riders, and maybe now you have that hundredth rider. Rarely does anything in life work across the board all the time.

6. There are certain things that, when said to a nervous or frightened rider, generally make matters worse. Don't feel embarrassed if they are things you've been saying all along; they're what most trainers *do* say, with the best of intentions. Try to substitute some items from the second list when you think your nervous rider needs support from you.

Avoid saying:

- "Relax." This means nothing to the nervous rider. No one can relax on command.

- "You'll do great!" Don't promise what you can't deliver. And doing "great" may be the thing of least importance to your rider at that moment.

- "Maybe this time you'll get a ribbon!" This stresses outcome over process and experience.

- "Oh, you're fine!" Don't bully a person's feeling. If a rider's nervous, let him be nervous. You're better off validating the person's feeling (whether or not you "agree" with it) than trying to override it with your preference for how he should feel.

Instead, try:

- Simply acknowledging or confirming the rider's anxious state. Validating her experience will go further in settling her down than trying to change it. Follow your rider's lead; if she looks nervous, ask her whether she is. You won't *cause* it by asking, and you just might relieve it considerably by letting her know that she doesn't need to keep it secret from you.

- Asking your rider to tell you what would be helpful for her at that moment. This takes you out of the guessing game and allows you to be more useful.

- Emphasizing process over outcome. Keep an active dialogue about the ongoing process of learning, and how setbacks, slumps, bad days, and bad trips are inherent and essential parts of this (and any) sport.

- Just standing by your rider, even silently, can often be of more support than saying something in a vain attempt to settle her. Your presence alone can be enough.

Be on the Lookout for:

- *Several of your students are manifesting the same type of problem.* This may be due to a blind spot, or a way of teaching or communicating that encourages a bad habit. It may also be an outgrowth of a personal issue that prevents you from teaching certain kinds of people as well as your skills would ordinarily allow (i.e., perhaps discomfort teaching people older than you are). Sometimes people with certain personality characteristics remind us consciously or subconsciously of those we used to know, and we automatically react to them the way we reacted to the others (an outspoken older male student reminds you of your overbearing dad, so you get defensive whenever the student asks a question about his lesson). If such "automatic reactions" happen frequently to you, they can affect how well you "see" a situation for what it really is or correctly deal with it. For example, a trainer who still smarts from not having been popular as a teenager may wind up with a barn full of adolescents who walk all over her during their lessons, because of her tendency to want to "fit in."

- *More than a few of your riders stop progressing at the very point where your level of riding has reached a plateau.* Maybe internal factors, like your own competitiveness, keep you from moving students along past your point of progress. Sometimes a student "protects" the trainer by masking her riding progress if she thinks it will make the trainer jealous or otherwise uncomfortable, or will make the trainers worry that the student may leave for a higher level trainer. Sometimes a rider subconsciously holds himself back so that he doesn't have to face the decision to move on.

- *More than a few of your riders become scared of riding, or find excuses to avoid getting on or taking their usual amount of lessons.* This could be a sign that your riders are feeling overfaced or overmounted. Go back over the things these people have said to you recently and see if there's any theme to them. For example, maybe there have been a lot of comments about how green the lesson horses are, or about how people wish that they had something "a little quieter." Even reviewing jokes made by your riders can be illuminating; group lesson riders joking nervously about who has to do a particular exercise first may be trying to tell their trainer that they don't yet feel up to the task. And, as always, if you're not certain about how your riders are feeling about their riding, their horses, or their training, ask them to tell you and then dialogue with them about their worries.

This ends this chapter on the psychology of teaching sport, in particular, riding. But since teaching is only one part—albeit a big one—of a trainer's job, the next chapter covers many of the other issues that professionals face in the industry. These include the influence of physical environments on mental attitude, dealing with money and customers, professional development, limit setting with boarders, communicating with clients, and similar concerns. The final chapter in this section covers work stress and the equestrian professional, and offers some ideas for identifying and reducing the sources of stress that come from dealing with all of the above.

Chapter Eleven

The Business of Being
a Riding Instructor or Trainer

BEING IN BUSINESS for yourself, or being largely responsible for your flow of clientele in someone else's barn, brings with it both large rewards and large headaches. Self-employed people face common challenges, whether they run a riding school, an equestrian training and breeding facility, a psychology practice, a law practice, or a grocery store. In its own way, each stretches the owner-manager's personal, professional, and business skills. And, sure enough, they tax these skills, too. But all of them also require the person in charge to learn to relate comfortably and effectively with a broad range of clientele, handle money transactions, set and maintain appropriate personal and business boundaries, and balance his or her sense of authority with sensitivity and character, among other things. People will always complain about the responsibility, the isolation from colleagues, and the long hours, but they do like the independence, the autonomy, and the pride that comes with running a good business. When things are working right, it's just grand.

This chapter speaks to these issues as they pertain to riding businesses. Sections on both professional-business aspects and on relationship aspects are included. A third section covers questions frequently asked of me by trainers.

Professional-Business Aspects

The Influence of Environment and Expectation

Never underestimate the power of environment and expectation to shape and sustain positive behaviors and attitudes in your clients. Years ago, a social psychologist conducted a fascinating experiment. Two subjects were instructed to sit in a room and wait for someone to hand over to each of them a sum of money. One of the subjects was told privately to expect to be given a dollar, and the other was told privately to expect ten cents. The person whose job it was to go into the room and hand each subject the money was given a dollar and a dime, but was not told which subject was to get which amount. This person went into the room, and eight times out of ten gave the dollar to the subject who was (silently) expecting to get the dollar, and gave the dime to the subject who (also silently) expected to get the ten cents.

Now, one would expect that by chance the money-giver would have gotten it "right" about half the time and "wrong" the other half. But getting the right amount to the right subject eight times out of ten is significantly better than random odds, and strongly suggests that the money-giver was influenced by some kind of nonverbal communication on the part of the two subjects about what each was expecting. Apparently, someone who is expecting a dollar looks or moves or acts differently from someone expecting a dime.

What meaning does this experiment have for running a riding business? It means that as an instructor, or trainer, or barn manager, you can bring out certain qualities in your students and other customers without lecture or comment but by orchestrating an atmosphere of horsemanship or social civility, or whatever, which, by itself, elicits certain attitudes on the part of the people within it. These attitudes can reflect self-respect or respect for peers and animals, dedication to the sport, a receptiveness toward learning, congeniality, or any other way of being that is what you want to have in your working environment. It is important to note that they come not from your manipulations of people but rather from your carriage and your demeanor and your expectations of how people should act and relate when at your barn. Your influence is quiet and subtle, nonverbal yet palpable. It is never frank or coercive. It is a way of being that invites a like way of being from others, but does not demand it.

I've been talking so far about creating the psychological environment, but the physical environment has a strong impact, too. Most barn owners and managers are already familiar with this aspect of running a good business and try to do the best they can with the time, money, and help they have. However, ignoring disorganized or unsightly grounds because there's nothing you feel you can do about it is no solution either. Better to do what you can anywhere you can than to surrender to the chaos and let your customers sense your hopelessness or indifference. A well-painted entrance sign, blankets folded, grooming equipment off the floor, soap at the sink, and toilet paper in the bathroom are within almost anybody's reach and communicate that you are mindful of the physical environment.

As an equestrian sport psychologist, I strongly believe that sloppy environs beget sloppy riding. It's hard to feel good about yourself or your riding if you can't feel good about the environment in which it's taking place. I'm not talking fancy or even pretty—just workmanlike and respectful toward the grandeur of the spirit of these horses we keep.

A client once related to me an interesting story about this. A dressage rider, she boarded at one barn and took her lessons at another. The moment her trailer hit the driveway of the lesson barn, she felt herself become a different rider: she told me that she felt more polished, acted more polished, and rode in a more polished fashion. The atmosphere, the structure, and the expectations that were part of that lesson barn triggered a psychological transformation that took place automatically. The result of that transformation was an immediate access to her very best riding.

With rare exception, she could never duplicate this feeling, or peak riding skill, at the barn where she boarded. The client told me how she never knew in whose tack trunk she might find her fly spray, or whether she'd find her horse in his stall or turned out, or how flooded the rings would be. By no means was it a bad place, and she was rather fond of the resident trainer. Nonetheless, all those irregularities served to chip away at her "polished" mindset. Sometimes she'd be able to recover her edge, but it was never easy and was always at the expense of her concentration and focus. She'd persevere anyway, and try to pretend that she was someplace else, or she'd dissociate—that is, disconnect—from the environment and ride out of a protective mental bubble that contained just her and her horse.

Well, you do what you can with the resources you have at different times in your life and learn to stretch yourself in whatever ways you need to reach your goals. This woman learned a lot from that experience about the importance of what's outside and around you, as well as what's inside. There is a lot that the former does for the latter.

Money Matters

Therapists used to think that the topic people most avoided in therapy was sex. Then they realized that people have even more trouble talking about money! Few other topics bring so quickly into boldface somebody's discomfort and issues about power, control, and identity. The handling of money in business speaks a loud, albeit cryptic, language.

What would money bugaboos look like in practice, specifically in a riding business? Any of the following plus a bunch of idiosyncratic others: undercharging for your services; chronic tardiness in getting out board bills or in collecting money; awkwardness in discussing your charges; or feeling overly gracious when accepting payment. That's not to say that everyone who does these things has an issue with money. Some people are so swamped trying to stay on top of everything that they're amazed they get the board bills out at all! But for others, the interpersonal management of money in general, or the putting of a dollar value on their expertise, brings with it a degree of unease.

When you set a fee schedule, you make a public statement about what you feel your worth as a professional is. Psychologically, it is a very bold move. This is one reason that it's difficult for many professionals (of any business) to state forthrightly their fees with the same ease with which they might give a new client directions to their place of business. I see this happen all the time with psychologists entering the field of private practice for the first time; they wrestle with how much to charge, then with how to state their fees to clients without looking quite so green about it, and then with how to deal with the anxiety of providing service commensurate with the fees stated.

There's something else about setting and stating fees, too: it tells people not only how valuable you believe your services are but where you view yourself in relation to other professionals in the community. You are essentially ranking yourself, which communicates a lot about your self-perception and self-esteem.

And then there are the ways in which somebody's money management causes funny things to happen in their relationships with customers. If you think about it abstractly for a moment, the transfer of money underscores an inequality of something in a relationship. Note that I'm saying an inequality of *something* and not of personal value, power, or control. The "thing" about which there's some inequality may be a command of a body of knowledge, an experience base, a service, or goods. The person getting the money has something that the payer wants or needs. It sounds simple enough, but consider for a moment some of the psychological or emotional ramifications. There are times when people will mistakenly tend to experience that inequality as one of power or control, rather than as one of service or expertise. The feeling the person then develops is: *If I pay you money for* xyz, *you are going to feel as if you have liberty to control* xyz *part of my life.* This feeling may have nothing to do with what's actually transpiring interpersonally between the one paying and the one receiving. In other words, Jane, an amateur who regularly teaches her daughter, may resent paying Hank, a professional, for his intermittent instruction of the daughter, both because of her fears that Hank will want to take over the daughter's training and because it emphasizes to her that she isn't "good enough" to train her daughter herself. Well, first of all, Hank may have no such notion, being very content with the current arrangement, and, second, Jane, being both an amateur instructor *and* the mother of the girl in question, probably isn't (nor should expect herself to be!) good enough, especially if riding aspirations are high. I use this vignette to illustrate that we can all be vulnerable at times to living out an interpersonal drama that is a creation entirely of our imagination.

Many people also use money to speak for them when they can't say what they want to say with words. Lots of times this is inadvertent or subconscious—the person isn't aware that he or she is using money as a means of communication. Delaying, reducing, or forgetting altogether about money owed is one way people manage to say, *I didn't like what I got,* or *I didn't get what I expected to get.* To paraphrase Freud, however, sometimes a late payment is just a late payment!

On the flip side of things, a trainer may have difficulty pressing a customer to settle a late account. Part of the discomfort is our socialization—it's "not nice" to ask people for money, even money duly owed you. But that kind of discomfort may be compounded by a trainer's issues about collecting money for his or her services. Self-doubts about your professional worth, a lack of confidence in how others recognize your expertise, or the absence of a well-formed professional self-image (not uncommon in newer, younger professionals) all make it harder to come right out and ask someone to pay up. If you are wrestling with one of these issues, and worry that it may be affecting your business, consider reading some self-help books on esteem-building or on developing business management skills, consulting informally with colleagues about how they handle uncomfortable money matters, talking things over with a mentor, or meeting for a few visits with a therapist who does work oriented toward helping people find practical solutions to problems.

Professional Identity as a Trainer or Riding Instructor

Many instructors tell me that they feel blessed to have made a career out of something they love as much as working around horses. I have heard the same thing from professional riders. Indeed, there is something special about making your livelihood through an activity that you'd opt to do, apart from work, for its inherent pleasure or satisfaction.

Being part of the equestrian community carries with it this good fortune but also some not so good issues as well. Few outsiders appreciate the physical wear and tear involved and the long hours required. In addition, trainers, farriers, stable help, barn managers, and people who make their living braiding, clipping, or shipping speak frequently of the lack of health and retirement benefits and the paucity of regulatory or certifying organizations that distinguish the competent from the incompetent. But one of the most difficult issues that people in the industry have to wrestle with is the public's (as well as their own) prejudiced perceptions of horse trainers and riding instructors and dealers. Despite the many virtues of the sport, and the many well-known people who have served as good statesmen and stateswomen, present-day professionals in this business are still shaking off the historical and sociocultural stereotype of "horse traders," with all its negative implications. For too many professionals, their business and their riding talents are not taken seriously by family members or certain non-horsey friends; their aspirations are still considered a "phase" before they truly settle down to a "real" (read, respectable) career. Many trainers have told me of being asked by their relatives at holiday dinners whether they're "still doing that horse thing." Does anybody ask such a question of the teacher or dental hygienist or attorney at the Thanksgiving table? They wouldn't dare.

It takes a lot of belief in yourself and a lot of mental stamina to keep ignoring this kind of dismissal of what one does for a living. Such blows to one's self-respect can take their toll in other ways, too, some that aren't always obvious. For instance, I think that some of the unidentifiable stress of being a professional in the equestrian industry is connected to this problem, whether or not one is personally affected. The issues that any community of professionals wrestles with resonate to some degree within each member. All lawyers are affected by bad lawyer jokes depicting them as sharks. All physicians are affected by some people's perception of them as greedy. Individuals within a professional community who personally experience this kind of conditional or mixed respect for what they do can really feel the blow to their professional self-esteem (how one feels about oneself) or self-image (how one sees or conceptualizes oneself).

There are antidotes to this sort of negative influence: a strong commitment to yourself despite external influence; camaraderie with other professionals in the industry; involvement in profession-related organizations at the local, regional, statewide, and national levels; candid discussions with those family members and friends who need to better understand and appreciate what riding means to you and that what you do for a livelihood and career is valid. I remember discussing the issue with a group of equestrian science majors at a local college. One young woman spoke of the chiding and lack of support she received for her choice of study from her family—except from her grandfather, who would tell her how proud he was of her devotion to and accomplishments in the equestrian field. He's the one to hang with, I told her, and suggested that she let him know just how much his support meant to her. Kudos to Grandpa!

Professional Development

The business of training horses and instructing riders does not (yet) require continuing education credits. Even if it did, credits would predominantly address—as they do in other professions—only the more academic dimensions of a trainer's or instructor's development, such as lesson planning, teaching strategies, business development. They wouldn't deal with the more personal aspects of being an equestrian professional. So how *do* people in the horse business go about rounding out their professional selves? Where do they learn "people" skills? How do they learn to build a personal training and business system that fits their individual needs? How do they accumulate the mass of personal wisdom through their work that will serve as an overarching, guiding philosophy about training, about horses, about people, about life?

A lot of trainers already feel a sense of contentment with how they have developed as professionals over the years, as well as about how they manage the public or social side of their riding operation. One may believe that he has excellent relationships with his riders and excellent problem-solving and communication skills; another may feel that her interpersonal skills are lacking but that she is a heck of a good teacher and doesn't care to become more accommodating and that's that. Both of these people are happy with where they are and the way in which things are working for them, and neither is more correct than the other. They do, though, have different priorities, and their teaching, training, and management styles will reflect them.

But many people in the business don't have a sense of "completion" regarding their professional selves and are looking for new or better answers. One, for example, may wish to be more patient in his teaching; another, more commanding in her presence at shows. One may want to be less anxious when discussing money matters with clients. And yet another wants to be more verbally supportive of her riders without allowing that to increase a sense of competition within the barn.

Creating an image of yourself as the professional you wish to become over the course of your career can function as a powerful first step toward moving in that direction. It offers a visual model (even if visual only in an imaginary sense) for you to map out the steps for achieving his or her goals. You can then learn the mental rehearsal skills taught in Chapter 4 to practice handling the situations with students, horse show officials, customers, or family members that currently cause you some discomfort. You can practice saying different things or responding to comments from others that typically leave you tongue-tied, or feeling as if you said a stupid thing once again. You can practice "walking around" in a new body that is taller, prouder, less self-conscious. You can mentally practice letting things roll off your back more easily or practice speaking up for yourself in those sticky professional situations where you find yourself unable to think fast enough.

There are other means, too, by which a person can begin to make changes. Reading is one. There are always any number of well-written books about self-development in libraries and bookstores. Ask colleagues if they ever think about these things—about their own development as trainers or as businesspeople, their styles of resolving differences with students, their ways of engendering good sportsmanship among their riders. Don't limit yourself to those from your own discipline of riding; speak to an uncle who works in racing, for instance, and ask him how he learned to feel comfortable when discussing money with his clients. Or approach your trainer-mentor from years back for tips on confidently and authoritatively advising customers who are twice your age.

Can you go to more workshops and seminars offered by horse-related organizations? If you do, be active when you're there and ask good questions. "Cross-educate": if you are a dressage instructor who hears of a conference on saddle-seat riding, check over the program and see if there is anything, say, on working with the very young student, or with the adult who is returning to the sport after a long hiatus. Consider consulting briefly with a good therapist to figure out how to be more assertive or more patient or otherwise expand your repertiore of communication skills. Apprentice yourself to a senior trainer or instructor whose work and manner you respect. Do it for a week, for one Tuesday every month for one season, or even for one day at a horse show. Watch and absorb. Learn as much as you can from your own experiences, too—you can be your own best teacher and guide. Reflect on your business day, on the interactions that took place, and on your handling of situations that came up with students, parents of students, and other customers. What did you like about your management of the situations? What would you have liked to happen differently and how might you have encouraged that? How do you think others feel about your interactions with them that day? You can keep a journal, or, if you're like most people with little down time during your day, you can just think quietly and informally about these things when you're bringing the horses in, sweeping the aisles at night, or walking out to your car to go home.

Professional Relations

The Business of Boundaries: What's Mine, What's Yours, What's Ours

You want to have some quiet moments in your office at the end of your day, but it has been taken over once again by a gaggle of girls sipping sodas and cleaning their tack on your desk. You've asked Beth's dad not to interrupt you with questions during Beth's lessons, but he continues to do so anyway. Two of your adult amateur riders persist in calling you at home after hours to discuss nonurgent business matters because that is the time that suits them.

On the other hand, perhaps, you discover that quite a few of your riders are uncomfortable discussing their riding programs and goals with you in other than the most formal of settings. Or that they don't feel they can ask your opinion about changing some part of their program. Or that they don't feel they can let you know of the days when they're sad or discouraged or angry or feel like giving up.

Both types of situations reflect problems with boundaries. The first set reflects boundaries that are loose, where the lines have become blurred between professional and friend and there aren't clear ideas about what (referring to role or time or place or situation) is managed or controlled by whom. In the second set, however, these boundaries are too rigid. They seem to have resulted in a formal and overly distant way of relating between professional and client. Neither is necessarily wrong; every professional is entitled to run his or her business and relationships in whatever way he or she sees fit. But figuring out how familiar or how formal to be with clients doesn't always come easily, especially in the riding industry, where you spend so much time together, may travel together, so strongly share common goals, and see each other at your worst (4 A.M.) and best. The style of the trainer will determine some of this, as certain people are more or less comfortable with varying degrees of informality and formality. And some businesses lend themselves to a less formal structure (a summer riding camp for kids) or more formal (an international level show or sales barn).

There is a difference, however, between the formality (or informality) with which a trainer or instructor relates to his or her clientele and the formality with which a barn is run or structured. Some trainers try to relate warmly and informally to their clients but wind up losing control over their barn. It's hard to feel you're captain of your ship when everyone and her mother is using your business phone, borrowing the barn's clippers, ignoring protocols for putting away tack and equipment, or showing up late for lessons. *That's* not friendly and informal; that's chaos.

You don't have to forfeit relatability though to have a smooth-running operation. Learning to relate openly and warmly to clientele *and* command respect for how you want things to be done around the barn is a skill that is often developed over time. If you want to learn it better, observe those who look as if they have it down. Watch how they act with clients and how they run their barn. Also watch how they handle situations in which they need to assert limits, such as dealing with customers who don't observe barn policies.

Two criteria for establishing the kind of working relationships and working atmosphere you want to have around your facility are how well it works for business and how right it feels to you. You'll get a reading on each if you give yourself the time to think about it and heed your gut reaction to what goes on around you. If you're annoyed at the way things are happening around you, trust that there's *something* wrong. That doesn't mean you haven't had *your* hand in allowing or creating the situation that's become troubling, but your feelings

about it are your best and most honest guides to what you need to change. You can figure out what to do differently to make things better. If you are feeling very distant from your riders, or alienated from them, trust that something is keeping you and them from coming together in a meaningful way. The problem could be you or them or both, but *whose* problem it is matters less—at least for the moment—than your awareness that something's amiss.

Comfort with Authority and Its Influence on the Way a Trainer Sets Boundaries

Some difficulties that trainers have in setting appropriate limits and personal boundaries with their clientele may come, in part, from their discomfort with being the expert, or authority, in the operation. This may seem an odd idea at first, but it is a common issue for many people in all walks of life. Many of us have some anxiety about being a recognized expert in an area in our life, especially in a public or very social setting. Some worry that they won't be up to snuff and will disappoint others, or that everyone will discover that they're just an imposter in this industry. Some feel too modest or think that they need at least to feign modesty. Others actually do feel pretty good about themselves in an authoritative role but are simply shy or embarrassed about assuming the role of "professional" riding instructor or trainer. In such cases, the trainer may run his or her barn, or even instruct, with tentativeness. He or she may also be reluctant to push a student in a certain direction, or to assume the confident demeanor that elicits excellent riding from pupils.

There are also trainers who are all *too* comfortable with their authority as professionals. They may alienate students and students' families by being too aggressive, by seeming unapproachable, or by not being open to discussion on various riding or personal issues. Ruling the roost in your own barn is important, but keep in mind that benign monarchs have always been able to get more out of their constituents than have aloof totalitarian rulers.

Dealing With Riders' Nonriding Problems

Sometimes, a trainer is talking with one of her riders about what seemed like a riding problem and suddenly realizes that she's not so sure it's really a "riding" problem after all. She thinks to herself, *This may be a personal problem or a family problem or a parent-child problem or a work-related problem. Whatever it is it doesn't really have to do with riding.* And, in fact, tensions in the home, workplace, or school do often affect a rider's mood or ability to concentrate, patience level, body tension level, or relationships with a trainer or barn buddies. So, what should this trainer do? Well, there really are only two things you can do. You can:

Say absolutely nothing, and hope that the matter will resolve itself or that the student will figure out that what seemed a riding problem is actually a symptom of something else. In the meantime, be supportive and patient; besides that being a kind gesture, it leaves a door open for the student to come to you and talk more candidly if he or she wishes.

Or:

Respectfully, tentatively, and sympathetically say a few words about thinking that something has seemed off in your student's riding for a while, and you wondered whether there were other things going on in his life that were distracting him. Be sensitive to cues on your student's part that he either wishes to discuss this further with you or emphatically doesn't.

Which is better? It depends on the situation. Below are listed a few criteria that can help you decide which way to move in such predicaments:

- how well you and the rider know each other;
- the degree to which the problem is affecting the student's riding;
- how comfortable you are when delving into a student's personal or private affairs;
- how receptive you expect the student to be to what you may say;

- the potential value of saying something directly to the point versus the risk of offending, embarrassing, or angering the student.

This issue came up at a workshop I taught where an attendee, a trainer, brought up an important point. She knew that she wasn't a psychologist and didn't want to have to function as one. Her job responsibilities, she said, were extensive enough! I agreed with her completely, and emphasized that this isn't about being anyone's therapist or having the diagnostic skills of one. Rather, it is about being sensitive to the problems of living that all of us face and acknowledging they they do affect our work and our play, and how specifically they may touch upon the riding of students with whom you closely work. The idea is never for you, as trainer, to solve your clients' problems. You won't know about most of them, anyway. The idea is to allow others their humanity, and to show yours. Riding isn't always only about riding. Think of the situation as similar to your spotting what you think is a veterinary or equine dental problem. You may pursue your hunch informally, but if the situation looks at all serious, you'll suggest the client follow a veterinarian's or dentist's recommendations.

What If Something Really Looks Awry?

There are times when a trainer recognizes signs of trouble in a rider that are worrisome apart from how they may be affecting her riding. Often, this happens with junior riders, when a trainer feels a greater sense of responsibility than with adult riders. Some signs of trouble that could warrant action include:

— significant changes in riding habits or in level of interest;

— increased aggressiveness, argumentativeness, or competitiveness with peers;

— sudden loss of a competitive edge;

— noticeable withdrawal from peers;

— excessive tearfulness during lessons or shows;

— despairing attitudes about ever improving or resolving a problem with the horse or pony;

— obvious (too public) and excessive conflicts with family members about riding, showing, grooming, etc.

If it's bad enough to be noticeable to everyone around, or looks serious enough to be worrisome, and you feel you can't *not* say or do something, take the youngster aside. Privately and nonjudgmentally explain that you've noticed certain changes and that you are worried and want to make sure she is getting the support or help needed. Has she herself noticed these changes? Have her parents? Has she talked to anyone about what's on her mind? Would she like you to mention to her parents that you've noticed certain changes just to get the ball rolling toward resolving the problem?

If you are so worried that you don't feel you should keep the matter between yourself and the child, explain to her that, though she might rather you not say anything to Mom and Dad, you think it wrong not to do so. Tell her that you want to share some of your observations with the parents, and then ask whether she would prefer to be there with you or prefer that you speak to them alone. Then, be good to your word. If you speak to the parents without the child present, be sure to give her some feedback on the discussion. Don't assume that the parents will do that on their own; I have found that they often leave that up to the "other" person—in this case, you—and the kid is left not knowing what is going on or who is thinking what.

Taking the Initiative to Communicate

One of the most valuable things a trainer can do to foster, maintain, and patch up relationships with clients and employees is to make a commitment to encouraging communication with them. Rather than waiting for *them* to bring to your attention a concern that they have or that the two of you are aware exists (but that no one has spoken openly about), consider bringing up the matter to them. People often get into trouble when "bringing things up" if they do so defensively, or with the idea that the other person is doing something wrong and you have to "point it out" to him. If instead you approach him in a spirit of "something is amiss here and I want us together to figure out what it is and move past it," you can have a conversation

that will feel good to both parties and create a feeling of teamsman-
ship. Remember, I'm not talking about Big Deal Talks; just chats that
you initiate with your riders, their family members, and your employees that enable you to keep a clear reading on how things are going
before they become messy.

Trainers can do this casually on an intermittent basis, or can create
more structured forums for talking, for instance, by making a point to
touch base with each student once a month. Another idea is to organize an informal snacks or soda or coffee hour in the tack room or
office every few weeks. No agenda is necessary; the objective is simply
to increase the amount of casual talk time you have with one another
and to create opportunities for conversation—so that you and the
client become a team, and so that rough spots can be addressed early
on, at a manageable stage, before they require "special handling."

Tips on Working Things Out

- Avoid getting stuck in keeping secrets between members of a
  family. If parents come to you because they're concerned
  about the effects of intense training on their daughter's
  moods, ask that the daughter be part of the conversation.
  Adults often underestimate the degree to which their kids are
  attuned to their worries and to the nature of conversations
  they have with trainers (or teachers, coaches, and the like).
  They are often much better off if they let their daughter or
  son in on their thinking and make them part of the change
  process. Excluding kids—especially adolescents—from such
  events does them a disservice; it further discourages the young
  rider from adopting a mature, active, and responsible role in
  evaluating the effect of training and competition on his
  moods, schoolwork, relationships, or anything else. Matters
  regarding secrecy and openness are often simpler when it involves kids of the same age group. Let's say one sibling in a
  riding family complains privately to you about his sister always
  making fun of his more plain pony. Ask if it would be OK if
  you spoke with the sister about his hurt feelings. Certain other

situations will be sensitive judgment calls—a fifteen-year-old rider confiding in you about family tensions that make it hard for her to concentrate on her riding, or an eight-year-old rider who mentions in passing that he feels sad all the time. Don't dismiss these confidences—it says a lot about you that your riders trust you enough to tell you things that are usually difficult to share. Assure the riders that you are really glad that they chose to tell you about these things, and that you'd like to be helpful, *and then ask how you may be able to do that.* Don't be surprised if you occasionally run into a situation where it becomes necessary for you to speak out. You may have to intervene even if you risk losing the client. Examples of such situations are domineering parents destructively pushing their child to win, a teenager with a drug problem, or a child who has become so depressed that he spends all his time at the barn in tears. You may also occasionally face a situation that is over your head or beyond the scope of your involvement, but as an adult involved in the lives of minors you will sometimes be called upon to actively wrestle with questions of privacy and disclosure so that you end up acting in the best (overall, not just riding) interests of the child.

- If you have something important to communicate, think out what it is you want to say before you talk. What is the core, or essential, communication? Put together, ahead of time, one or two sentences that accurately express your thoughts about the matter. Don't worry about its sounding contrived—it's not the whole conversation you're planning ahead, just one or two lines. And the satisfaction of having communicated exactly what you want will more than make up for any verbal stiffness. The following is the type of thing I mean:

  ✔ Josie, for the last few weeks you've seemed uncomfortable around me. Is there something the matter, or something about your lessons that's not working for you?

  ✔ Maggie, I get the feeling that you think I'm asking too much of you in your riding. True?

✔ Nick, I know you've been talking to other trainers about your horses. Are you thinking about leaving and working with someone else? If so, let's talk about it.

✔ Julie, you look so miserable at each lesson—tell me, what's going on?

✔ Lou, I really like having you in my barn, but I can't have you speaking negatively of me behind my back. Tell me straight what you're unhappy about and let's see if we can't work things out better.

✔ Kristen, sometimes you get such a know-it-all look on your face that I end up feeling you don't want to hear a thing from me. What *are* you thinking behind that look?

• Hear the other person out to the end once you start talking. Bite your tongue if you have to—you'll always get your chance to speak, correct the person, or defend yourself if need be. There's something about being given the opportunity to be heard that makes you better able to listen in turn. Under no circumstances, though, does this mean you should tolerate disrespect. If that crops up, calmly tell the other person that you don't wish to continue discussing things at that time.

• Try to be sensitive to your students' abilities to do what you think they are ready to do. You may be 100 percent correct that they are up to the task in front of them, but if they don't feel the same way, you have the potential for problems or, worse yet, an accident. Reality is a relative thing, and your perception of readiness in a student may be both right (in terms of skill level) and not right (in terms of what's inside the head of the rider). Negotiate (this does not mean argue!) with your rider as you would any other difference of ideas, and be willing to err on the side of the rider's perceptions unless you feel that in this instance encouragement and a push are more appropriate than support.

Working with the Parents of Your Junior Riders

Forging a Sense of Teamwork

Most kids come with a couple of parents in tow, so you can figure it's pretty much a package deal. It's much the same thing when I work with child clients in my practice. To me, the parents are part of the team, and they can offer valuable input, feedback, and support for the child and the program.

I'm also aware that it's not always easy to establish an ideal working alliance, whether we're talking about therapy or riding instruction. Some trainers want more involvement than a parent is willing or able to give; the parent drops the kid off at the barn day after day and comes back a few hours later to pick her up and has yet to get out of the car. This is a problem. That parent has no idea what's happening with the child's riding or how she is fitting in at the barn. The trainer feels dumped on for supervising the child on the grounds or for having to develop alone a riding program that's suitable for her. Everyone is disconnected and operating as independent units. And what about the child? Can she really feel that her parents are interested, or proud, or involved? Many kids would gladly trade in the parent's lack of interest for overconcern; despite their protestations, it's by far the lesser of the two evils and at least informs them that they're cared about.

Sometimes I have a similar situation develop with a child client. I may start to feel the parents are content just to drop off their kid and have me "fix" him in their absence and without their involvement. As soon as I sense this, I make structural changes in the therapy, such as altering the format to include more family sessions. I generally work with whole families anyway when I have a child client, because I don't like the child to feel as if he is the only one with the problem. I encourage the family to see any one person's distress or difficulty as part of what they all must try to help, collectively and empathically. Also, changes within families and within individuals happen much more quickly when you have all the players in the consulting room with you. Sometimes I invite Grandma and Grandpa to join a few sessions, too. Sometimes even a special aunt or uncle can be helpful—these people are frequently important figures in how a family operates and often have great ideas about how to change things. By now, it's generally accepted that you get more cooperation from people when they feel they are part of figuring out the solution. Many parents are very willing to get involved when they are approached in this way and don't feel imposed upon; rather, they appreciate their perspective and input being valued and taken into account.

Perhaps some of these ideas can be useful to you with your uninvolved parents. But if you find that you have lots of uninvolved parents, consider whether something in the way you handle things is disenfranchising the parents at your barn. Maybe some of them don't really feel welcome despite your saying they are. Maybe some feel that their input wouldn't be valued. Maybe those who aren't horse savvy are afraid that there's "no place" for them around the barn or in the training program. Maybe some are intimidated. Give these ideas some serious thought if you discover that the parent piece of your business doesn't go as smoothly as the rest.

Sometimes trainers will say to me, "Oh, yeah, I do that. I ask my kids' parents what they think . . . but they really don't say much." Remember that some parents are by nature more reserved in their thoughts and opinions, others may be too shy to say anything, others may not trust that their uneducated suggestions would count for much in contrast to a professional's. Some just don't have anything to say. But there may be others who don't feel invited to speak up and think that when the trainer asks their opinions, he's just being courteous. It's helpful for these parents if the trainer responds at the time to good ideas or constructive feedback—*"That is really helpful for me to hear, Mary. Your daughter doesn't often share with me what she's thinking after her lessons, so this gives me a better sense of what she feels she's ready for now."* Or *"I've been wondering if David was feeling overwhelmed with having two new ponies to get used to at the same time. I thought he might not want to say anything for fear you and his dad or I would have him put one on hold. I'm glad you filled me in on this. Let's figure out what the best next step will be."*

And what about the too-involved parents? If they tend to be intrusive with their opinions and comments, a trainer may try building in regular, periodic consultations so that there is an established forum for them to discuss things with you. This kind of structuring often precludes any intrusiveness because the parents know there is a designated time and place where they will be able to brings things up. Also, if you think there is some grumbling going on underfoot, approach the parents first rather than waiting for them to come to you. This way you are not caught off guard, the discussion doesn't take place in the wrong context (at the in-gate) or in front of people (the child, perhaps, or other clients, or prospective customers) that make you uncomfortable. Not only do you get to decide the where and when of things; you are communicating that you are not skittish about parents' concerns or dissatisfactions and that you are willing to hear them out. You are making an important statement both about being on top of things in your barn *and* about being receptive to client's concerns.

Limit-Setting Where Necessary

Occasionally, parents need help in recognizing what is your turf and what is theirs. The following are some ideas for what you might say to a parent in such circumstances. Remember that if you communicate an appreciation of their efforts to be involved and helpful, even when what they've offered has been less than useful, it does make it easier for them to hear what it is you are saying.

- I know you want to be helpful, Mr. Dole, but when Laurie is in the ring, we both need you to be more in the background.

- I know you like to be involved, and I really like that in parents, but when Simon's actually competing, I need to have his full attention. How about if we make it a point to touch base at the show but not right before his classes?

- I understand your concern for your daughter's safety, Miriam, but I need you and your husband to feel confident of my ability to keep riding safe for her. If you don't feel I've been able to do that, then let's sit down together this week and discuss it further.

- Clay [CEO of his company], I know you're used to running the show, but here at the barn you need to let me be in the captain's seat. I welcome your input but need the liberty to use it selectively.

- I know you're trying to be helpful, Pam, but when you give Ellen advice about her riding before a class without consulting me, it makes it difficult for her. Come talk to me first—it'll work out better, I think.

And for those parents who are delightful to work with and who really partner themselves with you, *let them know.* Tell them directly that they are a pleasure to have on board, and that you really appreciate how involved they are and how they manage to make their involvement both supportive to their child and helpful to you.

Frequently Asked Questions from Trainers and Riding Instructors

How can I best deal with a fearful student?

The worst thing you can do when faced with a fearful student is to join in his or her attempts to ignore the fear. Being in cahoots with a student's denial and avoidance only serves to make a bigger monster out of what could otherwise be a manageable feeling.

In general, you are much better off helping an anxious or fearful rider come to terms with his nerves. Fear is a slippery creature and can outsmart most attempts to "nail" it. The harder you try to bury it, the harder it smacks you over the head by surprise when you least expect it (at state finals, the last movement of your test, cooling your horse out in a field).

Many psychologists speak of fear as being a second cousin to excitement. Physiologically this is true: both give rise to graduated degrees of the famous fight-or-flight response, where the body primes itself for protection, be it scooting out of the way of a runaway horse or avoiding the risk of embarrassment when giving a public speech. But *psychologically* there is an enormous difference! Seasoned athletes sometimes talk about being able to "transform" their fear or nervousness into a welcome excitement; as noted earlier, one professional baseball player learned to give new definition to his pregame palpitating heart. Whereas previously it had served to usher in a full-blown anxiety attack, now it became his cue that he was "ready" for the game. This is an enviable talent, but don't expect it from everyone. Sometimes people read about these pros changing (by virtue of experience, practice, or different coping or thinking styles) their fear into excitement and then wind up feeling bad about themselves because *they* can't do that. And so they're left not only feeling fearful, but depressed and inadequate as well.

If a rider is open about her fears, spend some time talking with her about them when she's off the horse. When did they start? Do they pertain only to one horse or does it happen on all the horses she rides? What precipitated the fear, or did it develop gradually? What are the rider's ideas about how best to deal with the problem? Remember, you don't have to resolve the problem for your rider; you only have to let her know that you are on her side.

Let's bust a big myth. Talking about fears will not make them worse. *Not* talking about them does that. Now, there will always be some students who don't want to talk about feeling afraid, because they really believe it will make things worse. Alternatively, talking just may not be their coping style. Respect this. It's their privilege to wrestle personal bugaboos in a style of their own choosing. There are many ways to skin this cat.

In all but a very few cases it's best not to have students try to override fears by immersing themselves in the feared situation (directing them to jump the feared height, ride the feared gait, mount the feared horse, etc.). First of all, it's dangerous; scared riders are accidents about to happen. After all, you'd never try to reschool a frightened horse by overfacing him with the feared situation until he acclimates to it (as if he ever would!). Why would it work any better to terrorize your students in this way? Moreover, some fears turn out to be rather well founded and deserving of our respect.

You're likely to be better off taking students back to the level at which they feel comfortable and reasonably confident, and then letting them work their way back up *under supervision*. Don't abandon your riders to practice over and over on their own after a few successful attempts; there's too great a risk of backsliding. If a scared rider makes a mistake again, it could bring any progress right back to square one, or worse. Better that you monitor your riders until they really feel up to speed again.

Sometimes, however, riders need to be encouraged or pushed. At those times they do need you to lead the way back, and this may involve anything from a good pep talk to your strongly urging a particular exercise. Experience, sensitivity, and good judgment will help you decide which situations to handle in this way and which to deal with in the softer ways. Also, some trainers may be more inclined, by personality, to approach these kinds of situations in one way as opposed to others, no matter what the specifics are. It simplifies certain aspects of dealing with this problem but complicates others.

What if my student and I disagree about the validity of the fear?

There really is no disagreement to be had; a student's fear should be a nondebatable issue. You're always going to be better off starting where your rider is; otherwise, you end up threatening both the rapport with the student and the student's safety. If a rider feels the situation to be dangerous, then it has become so, either because it is or because the rider's uncertainty and anxiety have made it so. Logic never rules our emotions and physiology.

Also, think about it this way: we all know that we need our horses to carry the rhythm; they must be the ones taking us forward. It's no different with riders in their relationships with their trainers. The riders need to be carrying the forward momentum, not the trainer on the ground (figuratively) clucking. Once the trainer starts *pulling* her riders onward instead of *inspiring* them, those students are going to get awfully heavy.

Some of my young teenage riders are difficult for me to deal with during their lessons. They have started to act like know-it-alls, and don't seem to respect my instruction as much as before. What's happened, and what can I do about it?

There could be a couple of reasons for this, but I'll mention two of the more common ones. The first is a reflection of how comfortable the trainer is with his or her authority and with setting limits around the barn and in regard to barn behavior. As kids move from childhood proper into adolescence, they test the limits of acceptable behavior and of the authority of the adult figures around them. If a person is uncomfortable with saying *no* to certain things, or being firm with rules, then this is the point at which he'll feel his control slipping away. These kids, now thirteen, fourteen, will find it funny to throw the adult for a loop. It's not often that they can get one to feel as foolish and awkward and self-conscious as they feel, so they just love it when they can do that. And they will do it at almost any chance given them, and especially in a group or other public setting. As a trainer wrestling with this problem, you need to ask yourself if setting limits, communicating a sense of authority, or otherwise commanding respect from others is a weak point for you. If it is, try to counteract it by being aware of the tendency not to be firm enough, and then challenging yourself to act differently. You don't have to become tough or gruff; just act as if you run the show—which you do.

A related point is that adolescents are very good at making certain adults feel nervous and nearly as tongue-tied as they. Many adults respond to this by becoming solicitous of adolescents' favors; they try to make friends by being "nicer." This plays right into the teenager's hands and ultimately makes the situation, and imbalance of power, worse.

The second reason you may feel you are losing control over your adolescent riders stems from developmental considerations, and this has almost nothing to do with what you are or aren't doing. When kids move into adolescence, they unwittingly become involved in certain psychological conflicts—for instance, they both want independence and are afraid of it; they both hate having to rely on adults but are comforted by them; they seek more control but don't yet know how to wield it constructively. It's sometimes downright miserable, being fifteen. Many of the control battles manifesting themselves between you and your riders are no different from the battles these kids are having with their parents and their teachers. As a trainer, you too represent an authority figure, and therefore serve as the perfect foil for them to act out these internal issues. Teenagers will move in and out of relationship with you, will test your authority, and will one day need all the support from you that they can get—and the next day act as if they have trained themselves without so much as a comment from you. Don't take it personally, and remember that we once tortured those around us in very much the same way.

One of my younger riders approached me privately and told me that she feels her parents are pushing her too hard to ride. She doesn't want me to say anything to them. What should I do?

Yikes, a toughie; this question comes in many different colors. The kid says, *I want to play soccer sometimes, like my friends.* Or *My mom and dad fight about the money my riding is costing.* Or *I don't want a new pony, I like my Smokey. But my mom wants me to have a new one.* Or *I'm scared to do the bigger divisions but I don't want to make my parents mad at me but please don't tell them that I told you that . . .*

First off, tell your young rider that you're really glad that she let you know what's on her mind and that you'd like to help. Don't try to talk her out of how she feels; let the kid have her personal response to a situation. Don't tell her not to worry. Don't tell her what you don't know—for instance, that her parents aren't fighting about money or that her parents wouldn't be disappointed. Maybe they are fighting. Maybe they would be disappointed. Maybe they don't want to be fighting about money, or don't want to be the type who would be disappointed but can't help how they feel. And kids are very good at picking up innuendoes, so it's all too possible that the kid is right on target.

Try to understand the way the child is feeling and then communicate that to her directly. *(I can imagine what it's like to think of having to give up Smokey; he's been your buddy for years! And all for this another pony that you don't even know.)* Don't promise that the new pony will be better, or that she won't be scared once she starts doing the next division, or that she won't like soccer half as much as she likes riding. Ask her how you can help her with this problem, and find out why she doesn't want you to talk to her parents. Ask whether the four of you could talk together about this, or encourage her to mention it to her folks herself. Avoid getting caught in the middle of a situation like this; it's really not yours to solve. Try to see yourself more as midwifing the communication process between child and parent so that they can arrive at a resolution.

There's also the option of referring the family to a sports therapist for consultation. In fact, a lot of what comes through my office door looking at first like ordinary riding problems wind up being family miscommunication regarding goals or conflicting wishes, or people wanting certain things for others that the others aren't so sure they want. These situations usually can be quickly resolved, with the "riding" problem disappearing altogether.

What do I say at the in-gate to my nervous rider? Everything I've tried seems to backfire.

One of the best pieces of advice I can offer is not to try to talk someone out of what he is feeling but accept it as what it is. A few people do like to be distracted from their nervousness, but for others, someone trying to distract them only draws their attention more to what it is they are trying to forget about in the first place. Instead, try any of the following:

- Instead of telling your rider to relax, go ahead and acknowledge how he's feeling and smile supportively.

- Instead of saying, "You'll do great," ask your rider what he needs at that moment or what he would find it helpful for you to say.

- Focus your rider's attention on a positive riding reference experience from an earlier show or a recent lesson that can get her mentally oriented toward what she does well, and toward what she and her horse do successfully together. This can be an example of when your rider was finally able to softly and deeply sit the canter, or ride forward to the jumps, or find her diagonal without having to look down at her horse's shoulder.

- Orient your rider toward her riding resource room (see Chapter 8).

- Sing a silly song that becomes known as the "in-gate" song. This is a wonderful and effective technique that was brought to my attention by a trainer whose barnful of riders would crack up immediately upon hearing or singing their little ditty, called "The Weeny Man Song."

- Keep in mind that often your presence as trainer is sufficient. It can be enough for you to stand there next to your rider and wait with her. You don't always have to say something.

I have a parent who yells at her kid in front of others and at shows. It's a horrible situation, and I don't know what to do, or if I even have any business doing something about it. After all, it's her kid. Help!

It's my opinion that it is your business and you must intervene; it became your business when that child's parents asked you to be her trainer. Not only does it reflect poorly on your professionalism, but you're the one who must set the standard for how kids are motivated in your barn. The first thing you need to do is approach the parent during a quiet moment, preferably at the barn. Privacy is essential, and you probably should not speak in front of the child. Then tell the parent that although you can understand how this sport can make for a lot of frustrations, you cannot allow the child to be publicly humiliated, that it is nothing but destructive, and that it is not and never has been an accepted part of your training program. Tell the parent that it cannot happen again and that you will intervene in the future. Then *do it* if it does happen again: walk up to the two of them and tell the parent to stop. Step in between them if you have to. And, yes, be prepared to lose the client. No professional can ever be effective with a client if he feels he can't afford to lose the person. It's the same whether you are an attorney, a therapist, or a riding instructor. You must have faith in your overall rapport and history with the client or in your judgment of the situation.

What do I do with some parents who are too competitive at the barn?

You buy a dozen hobbyhorses and you hold a Parents' Horse Show. The parents all compete in a variety of classes with their kids serving as their trainers. Your barn manager is judge. Hysteria and caricature are strongly encouraged.

Chapter Twelve

Work Stress and the Trainer-Instructor

TRAINERS AND RIDING INSTRUCTORS face innumerable sources of stress in their work. With everyone so focused on helping the athlete perform better, however, little attention has been paid to the coaches on whom these athletes depend. This is as typical of the equestrian sports as it is of others.

As a trainer, you bear heavy loads. You are largely responsible for the overall care and maintenance of many of your owners' horses, and for developing a vision of where each rider or combination can expect to move in a season or a career. This responsibility is even greater if the rider is an active and serious competitor. You also often wind up bearing the brunt of a rider's or owner's disappointment and frustration, and sometimes unexpectedly find yourself in the middle of a family drama. Then there are the pressures associated with the training and showing of other peoples' horses, as well as with training and showing your own prospects. And all this doesn't even address concerns about the viability of your business, as well as the planning for *your* future—the other bugaboo of self-employment. Finding and keeping good help is another big worry for many, and the schedule demands are often problematic for those who have (or want) a social life or family. And don't forget the traveling and the physical labor involved in all that moving around, in addition to the day-to-day management of customers, riders, and support staff while on the road.

How Stress Can Show Up in Trainers

Many people recognize the more obvious signs of stress, but stress can also show up in ways that aren't quite so recognizable at first blush. Use the list below to spot indicators of stress that might have gone unidentified.

- Feelings of burnout that can result in boredom, irritability with riders and customers, lack of interest in lessons, lack of new lesson ideas, loss of excitement about riding or showing;

- Growing impatience with people, situations, or students' lack of progress that would not have bothered you previously;

- Negative changes in eating, health, grooming, or other self-care habits; excessive fatigue or depression;

- Excessive drinking, drug use;

- Finding yourself complaining about horse shows, customers, the industry in general more than usual (or more than you care to admit!);

- Increase in frequency or intensity of arguments with loved ones or customers;

- Students seeming bored or irritable, not progressing as expected, starting to challenge you inappropriately;

- Changes in your handling of horses (pushing them harder, becoming rougher, loss of compassion);

- Indoor, nine-to-five jobs starting to look real good

There's no big cause for alarm if these seem familiar; they *are* part of what has developed into a very stress-filled industry. And keep in mind that people feel stress even when nothing is "wrong." It's important, though, to recognize if you're experiencing more than your share of work-related stress, because it does reflect on you personally and professionally and can affect the moods and attitudes of those with whom you work. If you're experiencing these signs of stress very frequently, very intensely, or chronically—if you don't like your feelings in regard to your work and your dealings with people—you may want to take steps to change the situation.

What to Do Differently

This section offers a variety of ideas for what you might do differently in your business in order to diminish the stress. I know from speaking with many trainers that running a boarding, lesson, sales, or show barn can get very complicated at times, and that it has become harder and harder to stay on top of all ends of business and customer relations. I'm also aware that the financial pressures continue to rise at a very steep rate and make it a concern for low-, middle-, and high-profile trainers alike.

It's too obvious to say that when someone can make changes in how things are done, he or she should do so. Many times, the problem is that trainers feel helpless regarding any possibility for change in the high-stress parts of their work: "I *have* to teach late into the evening, because that's when my riders can come." "I *have* to take my customers to shows each weekend, or they'll find someone who will!" "Boarders want better hay but have a fit if I mention rising costs." "My teenaged riders are getting snarly with me, and I don't know if it's me or them; I dread their lessons now." "If I don't start pinning soon on this pre-green hunter, my customer will take it elsewhere and never look back." Even those trainers who do feel hopeful about making changes have trouble finding workable, practical, simple solutions to the myriad of situations needing remediation.

One instructor at a college riding program voiced her experience of students pressuring her to be more than just their riding instructor. She said during a seminar, "It's like they want me to be their mother!" The answer to this dilemma lay in both being firm about limits regarding her role and her availability to students, and in her understanding of the mentoring role these students ascribe to her on the heels of having recently left their families and friends and familiar environments for a college dorm. It's always helpful to balance the encouragement of mature behavior with sensitivity to the developmental hurdles these kids negotiate in creating lives for themselves in their new (parent-less) surroundings.

Another trainer spoke to me about feeling stressed over having to manage the growing competitiveness between a mother and daughter in her barn. They both shared a horse and plagued the trainer with questions about who the horse was going better for. I encouraged the trainer to open up a dialogue with them, either separately or together, about how they seem to be competing with each other for who was the better rider and to say that she's worried it might all catch up with them to the point where they don't enjoy riding together as much as before and wouldn't that be a shame. Often people restrain themselves from mentioning "the problem" to someone directly, but if you bring things up in a timely and supportive manner, it can be much more helpful than beating around the bush. Just because something is unspoken doesn't mean it's unfelt—I find that people are better off dealing as directly with an issue as they can, whether it's one within themselves or with someone else. For this trainer, however, it was important that she approach the mother and daughter from the same side of the fence, that is, as a collaborator trying to find solutions to an unpleasant situation, rather than as a criticizer of the relationship between mother and daughter.

So there *are* answers. Often, they can be found in nothing more than making a commitment to doing one thing—just one—differently. Making one change somewhere in the scheme of things can often lead to a feeling of: "OK, I'm doing something about this and I'll figure out the next best step later." That one little thing may be condensing your lesson schedule so that you can leave the barn a half hour earlier than usual on Tuesday nights. It may be an open letter to all your boarders explaining that you want to institute a certain, improved type of service but worry that they'll object to the necessary increase in fees. It may be consulting a psychologist or pediatrician, or anyone else who knows something about adolescent development, to find out how best to deal with a snarly teen. It may mean deciding to talk candidly to the owner of the horse that's not yet pinning and finding out exactly how she feels, so that there are no surprises waiting in the wings.

I often find that when certain situations feel locked or stuck, it almost matters less *what* somebody decides to do than that they decide to do *something*. In life or business, as in riding, making a wrong decision is never as bad as making none at all. It's the passivity and sense of defeat that really knocks you down when you see yourself doing nothing to change what has become unpleasant or, in some cases, downright untenable.

More Food for Thought

Can you possibly . . . ?

- Take at least some time out of an altogether too busy schedule and give some of these ideas more than a passing thought;

- Consider how you might create informal or organized forums for discussion at the barn for parents, families, or owners. Small groups over coffee and doughnuts? One-on-one catch-up chats? Making it a policy to meet personally with your customers once a month in your office—for instance, when they pay their bill—to check on frustrations, perceptions about progress, thoughts about the training regimen, and so on?

- What about setting up monthly or bimonthly family nights at the barn—casual evenings with pizza and soda when families can talk among themselves or with you about all sorts of things that you don't ordinarily have time for. You can get the talk going by asking them what was the hardest, easiest, most stressful, most surprising, most and least rewarding aspect of horse showing that month. To the degree that the stress you feel in your business is due to the relationship end of things, these ideas can make a significant difference. They at least indicate to your customers and staff that you are aware of their importance, even if you don't have answers all the time.

- Speak candidly with other trainers to see if they experience similar stress in their work. What do they do to manage things more easily? What has and hasn't worked? The only thing worse than feeling overly stressed is feeling overly stressed all by yourself. Some people worry that fellow professionals would be critical of them if they were honest about what they find difficult in the business, but I think it's more accurate to say that candor usually begets candor.

- Do something to treat yourself better: make a commitment to eat better, get a half hour more sleep a night, take ten minutes before going to sleep to read, learn to meditate or do yoga. Any of these things can make you feel that you're not victim to your lifestyle but have some control over doing something different.

Just to recap, use the following guidelines for making changes in your professional life to reduce stress:

1. Commit to the idea of doing something about a problem that is different from how you are trying to solve it now.

2. Put responsibility where it belongs by engaging your customers in some of the decisions around the barn that will directly affect them.

3. Agree with your riders on some mid- to long-term plans, and reassess their suitability at regular intervals.

4. Begin the practice of having regular, candid conversations with customers and students. Remember, everyone does better when he feels he's being heard. People *want* relationships.

5. Develop peer relationships with other trainers and instructors which are characterized by candor and mutual support, not bravado. Consider, too, turning to senior, well-respected figures in the field as mentors. You don't have to carve out your career all by yourself.

Some Thoughts on Dealing Specifically with Performance Demands and Anxieties

For many trainers, showing customers' horses constitutes a significant part of their job and is a major contributor to stress. This section was written with them in mind. It describes some specific mental strategies that competitive amateur and professional athletes from all sports use successfully to deal with performance anxiety.

Our minds give us dreams and fantasies and other creations that aren't exactly "real life" real. Why not take advantage of this to spring free from logic in order to enhance your riding? Consider how jumps can look at least a foot taller than they really are on days when you don't feel confident or when your horse isn't going well. Then think about how inviting they look when you and your horse are in synch. Outside things stay the same, but from the inside it can all *seem* different. It all depends on how you are feeling or thinking about yourself at the time. This curious phenomenon—that is, the ability to alter your perceptual, internal experience apart from external sensory reality—hasn't gone unnoticed by sport psychologists and has become one of the greatest tools in helping athletes transform their inner experiences before and during "game time."

One of the most common of these manipulable inner experiences is what is often called *tunnel vision,* an extraordinary tool for the professional and amateur alike. Tunnel vision is the experiential phenomenon of being aware of only that which is immediately relevant to the task at hand. That means, seeing what you need to see *and only that,* feeling or sensing in your body and your horse's body and movement everything you need to feel *and only that,* concentrating solely and intensively on exactly what you are doing, what you will need to be doing in the next moment, what you will need to think about doing soon, and so on. Nothing distracts you, nothing sidewinds you, nothing flusters you. You just go. You take no notice of who's at the show, who's watching by the rail, who's observing you in the schooling area. It's just you and your horse and the job at hand.

A close cousin to tunnel vision is the psychological phenomenon called *dissociation.* This is sometimes described as a subtle feeling of physical or emotional detachment from the immediate goings-on. You are aware that the owner of the horse you are riding is sitting in the bleachers, but that seems to have nothing to do with what you are feeling or thinking or doing. You are aware that the horse warmed up brilliantly and you could win the class, but it does nothing to change how you are going to ride him. You are aware as you stand at the in-gate waiting to ride that you have to get a sale horse from your barn to another's by 4 P.M. that afternoon, but time has lost its meaning for the moment. Again, although the psychological experience of dissociation is a little different, it's just you and your horse and the job at hand. The tennis great Arthur Ashe called it "playing in the zone," a feeling when you know you're right on with your game and have all your athletic (or creative or mental) abilities at your disposal. Ted Williams, one of the greatest baseball hitters of all time, used to say that when he was in this zone, the pitches would seem to come to him so slowly that he could see the stitches on the ball. Though physiologically impossible, that perception was Williams's momentary reality. It's no wonder the man made contact as often as he did.

These kinds of mental experiences happen to really good athletes on a regular basis. It's a direct result of their mental practice and preparation, although over time the prep can take place in a matter of moments rather than minutes. How do these athletes get these experiences to happen consistently and without strain? First, they learn to identify them when they are happening naturally, without any effort, whether or not they happen in riding contexts. For instance, sometimes we can catch ourselves being so totally absorbed in something that we don't notice all that's going on around us. Think, for a moment, of a time when you were so absorbed in a good movie on TV that you didn't hear the phone ring. That's an example of natural tunnel vision. An example of a natural dissociation is when someone gets an upsetting phone call but is then able to detach herself from the troublesome situation to finish a report that's due the next day at school or at work. While these aren't riding examples, recognizing them underscores that you probably already have some history with them. You don't have to start from scratch in developing the capacity for tunnel vision or dissociation, you just have to refine your ability and learn to apply it to your riding.

Once you've identified times when you've experienced these phenomena, then identify the variables, either in the environment or in your psychological state, that contributed to their occurrence. What was different about how you were feeling or how you were approaching a task? What were the external conditions, and did they include the presence of certain people? Were certain people absent, and is *that* usually associated with such experiences? Then see if you can come up with times when you may have experienced tunnel vision or dissociation while riding. Ask yourself these questions, plus others. For example, was there something different about how your day started, how your horse warmed up, your attitude or mood, or how you and your trainer or daughter or husband or wife were getting along?

The goal is to be able to summon up the experiences at will, from your memory bank, or from your capacity to effect immediate psychological or physiological changes within yourself. After a while, these experiences can become a regular part of your overall mind set while riding or during certain parts of your ride.

Let me give you an example of how I use another mental phenomenon, *time expansion,* to help my riding. Time expansion allows you to slow down your subjective experience of time passing. With practice, I have learned to slow my sense of time so that I don't feel it rushing by me too fast, which sometimes causes me to ride impulsively and make poor decisions. But I'm not at risk for rushing my rides all the time, only at certain times, like coming out of a turn toward a fence set close to the turn, or approaching a large combination of jumps. That's when I now benefit from expanding my perception of time passage so that I feel as if I have all the time that I need to think and respond to my horse, stride by stride. What is eliminated is that horrible sensation of *Hurry up, Janet, and do something anything, maybe try a bend—no, better a half-halt—no, get him forward omigosh there's no time to do anything now because we're two feet from the jump.* Instead, my inner experience is *OK, what do we need here . . . just keep him moving forward and let the pace buy the jump, oops watch his left bulge, that's better, now just sit chilly to the fence.* Do I need to tell you which is more pleasant, not to mention effective?

How did I learn to do this? By identifying or remembering natural instances of subjectively slowed time passage (a boring classroom lecture where every minute felt like ten, waiting for a delayed train, waiting at the service station for my snow tires to be put on, and any other place where I've found myself muttering *This is taking forever*). I knew that these kinds of phenomena could happen for me, so I'd watch for when they would happen while I was riding—a glimmer here or there at first; maybe one lesson where I felt remarkably, surprisingly "unrushed" while cantering or jumping; maybe one round in a horse show where I remembered a delightful feeling of having ridden on "slow motion." Then I'd practice recapturing the experience, either through some mental rehearsal or self-hypnosis. And, finally, I'd practice generating new experiences of time expansion for future situations.

To summarize the steps you take in learning to develop these mental experiences:

Step One: Notice where, when, and under what environmental, social, and psychological conditions the targeted experience happens to you naturally.

Step Two: Practice summoning up the experience in similar situations where it hasn't yet presented itself.

Step Three: Cultivate your ability to generate the experience at will through such techniques as mental rehearsal, self-hypnosis, relaxation, meditation, and the like.

The ability to pull up such mental phenomena (you can read more about this in Chapter 5, on hypnosis) and superimpose them on your experience of the moment can be a great psychological tool for the professional rider or trainer. They're useful in keeping at bay the anxieties that would otherwise creep up about people watching you ride or making sure everything is or looks perfect. It's as if you know that you're anxious, but you don't care. You may be aware that you'd like to impress some of the people around you, but you don't try to. You may have a dry throat, but it is a completely separate experience from the rest of you and from your attentions at that moment. That's what being "in the zone" can be like, and for any athlete—professional or amateur—in the stir of competition, it's a fabulous place to find yourself.

The Many Manifestations of Class

There's one more note about performance anxiety that I'd like to make in this chapter. There are many ways to present yourself well beside by winning. Class and professionalism always show through anyone's riding errors and point to qualities that often mean more to prospective clients than show-ring savvy or a certain level of riding expertise. In fact, I was initially drawn to my current trainer that very way. While he was schooling one of his students in the warm-up arena at a horse show, I heard him suggest that she avoid a portion of the arena that had been cordoned off by management. Despite the fact that all the other riders warming up their horses, plus all their trainers, were ignoring the cones and using the extra space, this one trainer said to his student that he didn't know why management had the area blocked off, but that they must have had a reason, so it should be respected. I didn't even know the man's name at the time, but what I heard told me a lot about his character and of his regard for other people's wishes whether or not they were there to witness his actions. That was the kind of person I was interested in working with, and so, having been on the look-out for a trainer, I approached him for help at that very show. The relationship has panned out marvelously. Have some faith in doing what you know to be right in these situations, rather than going along with the masses. It's a very attractive quality. Besides, your mother would be proud.

Part Three
For Everyone

Chapter Thirteen

To the Parents and Trainers of Young Riders

LIKE OTHER COMPETITIVE sports where opportunities for distinction, advancement, and elite status exist, and where national championships and even Olympic medals beckon, riding can bring out the best and the worst in the nature of its athletes and their entourages. We've all seen admirable acts of moral courage and sportsmanship. We've enjoyed watching kids with a good sense of responsibility, self-discipline, regard for their equine partners, balanced perspective on winning and losing, and a love of sport and challenge. All these things the equestrian sports can teach. But they can also teach less sportsmanlike lessons.

We have witnessed very young as well as older junior riders who have lost perspective on their riding and showing, who yell at their parents and trainers, mutter ugly things under their breath, alienate themselves from their peers, yank their horses, storm out of lessons. And then there are others whose inner distress shows up in a different way—they who ride, train, or show without joy, without interest anymore. They may go through the motions, but their hearts are no longer in it. In both situations, something is grossly amiss.

This chapter is written for the parents and instructors or trainers of young riders. Its purpose is to help them navigate successfully through some of the complex issues in the sport, such as cultivating sportsmanship, sustaining emotional health in intensely competitive environments, monitoring for overtraining and burnout, and monitoring (or self-monitoring) for parental over- or underinvolvement. These are critical matters that make a difference between having the sport add to one's life or take a horrible and psychologically costly toll.

The Potential Benefits of Sport

Athletics of any kind provide youngsters with innumerable benefits, besides being just plain fun. In fact, Eric Margenau, a sport psychologist and the author of *Sports Without Pressure,* discusses research suggesting that children who are exposed frequently to sports early in life are healthier physically and emotionally, and grow up to become healthier adults. Sport affords children (and grownups) the opportunity for physical activity that's vital to good overall health. There's something to be said, too, for the sense of mastery and confidence that comes from liking what your body can do, how it can balance, catch, run, and jump. Sport also provides opportunities for fantasy and escape that boost our psyches and relieve tension. Another important psychological benefit that sport bestows is the development of self-esteem. This happens through meeting the challenges of going out and learning something new, or doing something to the best of your ability. Other potential benefits for riders include the development and refinement of such psychological characteristics as the ability to plan ahead, cope with stress, empathize with others, assume responsibility for the care of a large animal, function somewhat independently, tolerate frustration, make decisions on one's own, and other valued qualities.

Not long ago, three sport psychologists who follow a psychoeducational-developmental perspective in their work with athletes assembled their own list of valuable skills learned by participation in sports:

ATHLETES' VALUABLE LIFE SKILLS

To perform under pressure
To be organized
To meet challenges
To handle both success and failure
To accept others' values and beliefs
To be flexible to succeed
To be patient

To take risks
To make a commitment and stick to it
To know how to win and how to lose
To work with people you don't necessarily like
To respect others
To have self-control
To push yourself to the limit
To recognize your limitations
To compete without hatred
To accept responsibility for your behavior
To be dedicated
To accept criticism and feedback as a part of learning
To evaluate yourself
To be flexible
To make good decisions
To set and attain goals
To communicate with others
To be able to learn
To work within a system
To be self-motivated

But as M. R. Weiss wisely points out in her chapter "Children in Sport: An Educational Model," the key term in all this talk about the value of sport is *potential benefits.* None of the benefits noted above is automatically transmitted to kids by their mere participation in sports. And this is especially so for some of the more sophisticated psychological qualities listed. Weiss discusses how important it is for parents, coaches, and sport psychologist consultants to work together to structure the sporting experiences in ways that maximize the realization of these benefits. With respect to riding, why shouldn't we encourage parents, junior riders, and their trainers to make these life skills a part of their ongoing dialogue as much as other objectives that are discussed? If we talk about the importance of developing a quieter seat or a better eye for distances, why can't we also stress sportsmanship, responsibility, tolerance of constructive criticism, and independent thinking as objectives?

One long-standing problem is finding a way to give these ideas more attention than just lip service. Instructors of young people will come up to me and say, "I really want my kids to be better at sports, but I don't know how to make that happen." One way to do this is to incorporate the ideas openly as part of the program, addressing them at regular intervals. Trainers can even select "themes" of the month, where kids are expected to undertake a project emphasizing their commitment to, let's say, being more responsible, more flexible, part of a system, or a good sport. Imagine, for instance, that the theme is teamwork. One rider volunteers to braid or groom once for another kid in the barn who wouldn't be able to go to an upcoming horse show due to a shortage of funds. Or, adding a little whimsy, everyone in the barn switches saddles for a week in the spirit of learning "flexibility." This little game is a metaphor—no one really believes that switching saddles for one week actually creates a more flexible psychology, but it does have everyone talking and joking about the game, the concept—and that's how it makes the difference. These things lift the idea of "building character" off the page and bring it to life.

Overtraining and Burnout

Many of the benefits outlined above get trampled when someone's enthusiasm and good intentions go awry. Believing that "more is better" and fueled by fears of being undertrained and underprepared, many training programs take on monstrous dimensions and extort ghastly tolls. Perpetrators include coaches, trainers, family members, and even the athletes themselves. It's no different in the equestrian sports.

What does overtraining look like and how can you identify it before it becomes a problem? Experts distinguish between burnout, or an athlete's feeling stale, and true overtraining syndrome. Burnout can show up as avoidance of training sessions or the barn itself, lack of effort at lessons or shows, a lackadaisical attitude about riding, irritability around the barn or during discussions about riding, an extended slackening off in performance, crying spells, impatience with one's horse or frequent battles of will, among others. The overtraining syndrome is farther along on the continuum and involves a variety of recognizable psychophysiological symptoms, such as hormonal changes, decreases in body weight and fat levels, chronic muscle soreness, changes in one's immune system, sleep disturbances, and increased vulnerability to injury and illness. Apathy, depression, anger, and fatigue also figure in the picture and may, to the casual observer, be mistaken for an "attitude problem." Early recognition and intervention are key to preserving the athlete's physical and mental health and his or her love of the sport.

I've had more than a few teenagers come through my office seeking help for what they believed was a "riding problem." They tell me that they are losing their nerve in lessons, their competitive edge at shows, and their belief in themselves as capable riders. They worry that their trainers are becoming increasingly frustrated with them, their parents disappointed, their horses impatient. They want from me a technique, some mental strategy that will make everything alright again. "Is there a visualization that I can do?" they beseech me. "A tape you can make?" "Something to make me ride better . . . ?" And I look at these kids and see in their faces that they're not happy anymore with what they're doing. They look overwhelmed; some look depressed. When I disclose my observations, they nod in self-recognition, or become tearful in the moment of self-discovery. "This isn't a 'riding' problem," I tell them. "It's another kind of problem, but your riding is OK." What happens to these kids is they feel an enormous sense of relief. They learn that their riding has not deteriorated in itself but instead has been compromised by matters related to having lost, somehow, their way in this sport. They then become better able to speak about the felt pressures and demands that have taken things over the edge for them. The solution subsequently lies in managing those issues directly by speaking to the parent and/or trainer with the idea of changing the program and diminishing the pressures to win, look good, do well, ride more, try harder. In each of these cases, no one was conceptualizing the problem as other than a technical riding problem—not the parent, not the trainer, not the kid. The equestrian community needs help in discriminating between skill-based problems and those springing from the worries someone might have about how her progress is measuring up to the hopes and ideals of herself or someone important to her.

For Parents: Tips on Preventing Burnout in the First Place

An ounce of prevention being worth a pound of cure is ever so true when it comes to sport and burnout. Use the tips below to avoid a burnout situation in your child or children to begin with, and instead foster an appreciation of sportsmanship and a love of the sense of mastery that comes from doing something competently, even if not victoriously.

- Avoid defining success and failure in terms of your child's winning and losing. Some people simply aren't aware of how frequently this comes out in what they say. "How's Cindy enjoying her new pony?" you overhear at the barn. "Great," is the reply, "she was champion with her at the show last week!" A simple answer from a proud or enthusiastic parent—but one bespeaking the value of winning. Notice that the question was about Cindy's enjoyment in the first place, and not her showing. This happens all the time and doesn't have to mean a big deal unless winning and losing at shows has become a pressure point. If that's the case, be careful about your choice of language and what you emphasize in conversation with your child or others and what you downplay.

- Do not coach! Your child has a coach—the trainer. Now let him or her do the job. What your child needs you to be is an unconditional fan. The last thing he needs or wants from you is technical or strategic advice. Just be his biggest fan—win or lose.

- Help make (and keep) riding fun for your child. The more fun the child has, the more she will learn. Besides, isn't that what she started riding for in the first place? The best defense against burnout is the child's regular and consistent enjoyment in what she is doing.

- Allow your child to fail and to be comfortable with failure. Fear of failing is a big stumbling block for many riders, one that keeps them from stretching their talent. It's also reasonable to think that learning to feel comfortable while trying something new, and while failing in one area of life (sport), can make it easier to do the same in other areas (social, academic, or, ultimately, business and career). Successful people don't shy away from opportunities where they might fail; they have learned either to take failure in stride or to pluck some valuable learning from the experience.

One family consulted with me to learn how to help Vicki, twelve, with her growing nervousness at shows. Vicki's nervousness turned out to be an outgrowth of her growing expectations of placing first each time out. Very competitive with her younger sister, who in turn was very competitive with her, Vicki's parents had tried to diminish this dynamic by encouraging their involvements in separate activities (for Vicki, riding, and for the sister, dance). This way, they figured, neither would ever be "outdone" by the other, and the competitiveness would cease. A well-intentioned decision no doubt but an unfortunate one, because what happened was that neither daughter learned how to be OK at being "outdone" by somebody else in any endeavor; it was first-or-bust for these kids. Imagine trying to do the children's hunters with that kind of pressure on yourself. Forget it. Once a child recognizes that there *is* life after a second or a fifth or a no-place finish, he or she is freer to get on and ride in a far more relaxed manner. Let your kids learn to be comfortable with not winning and you'll be doing them a great service.

- Never humiliate, degrade, or embarrass a child. It is one of the most damaging and unproductive things a parent can do. Nobody ever rode better, acted more appropriately, or thought more maturely out of a feeling of shame.

- All along, try to stress the process of participation over outcome. Emphasize the value of learning new skills, refining old ones, and having fun. But don't just give lip service to this; ask your child about the learning process and its ups and downs rather than orienting questions toward win or lose, best or worst, fastest or slowest. Choking under pressure is often caused by too narrow a focus on the immediate outcome of the performance.

- Never compare your child's progress with others'. Some parents who would swear they'd never do this find themselves doing just that when they are angry or frustrated. Be on the lookout for when you, as parent, may be likely to blurt something out you'd later regret. Also, be mindful of developmental differences; not all fifteen-year-olds have the same level of emotional maturity, physical coordination, or self-control.

- Love and accept your child unconditionally. Never punish him for a poor performance by withdrawing emotionally or responding with disgust or disapproval. If you do have such feelings, do everything in your power to keep them from view, and seek help in protecting your relationship with your son or daughter from your excessive investment in his or her performance. Here's a tasty story relayed by sport psychologist Dr. Alan Goldberg that touches on this very issue. In the 1988 Olympics in Seoul, Greg Louganis needed a perfect 10 on his last dive to overtake the Chinese diver for the gold medal. His last thought right before he went was: "If I don't make it, my mother will still love me." He won the gold.

For Trainers and Instructors: More Tips

Much of the above section for parents is important for trainers and instructors, especially the sections on avoiding humiliation tactics and on helping kids learn to fail with grace. Here are some other tips that can help make the difference between a kid who enjoys the whole shebang of riding and one who is likely to soon have one foot out the door.

- Deal with your riders as whole people by taking an interest in them beyond their riding. Ask about school, pets, their grandma, their winter vacation, their boyfriend. Even a casual inquiry makes a difference to the youngster in helping her feel less one-dimensional, more cared about. And why shouldn't kids want to feel like that? They *are* kids, after all. If they mention their personal problems, consider it an opportunity to enhance your relationship with them rather than a hassle or interference with "the program." Usually, kids aren't asking so much for specific advice as for support, interpersonal contact, and someone to listen.

- Challenge each rider to stretch in his abilities, but refrain always from using threats. The prospect of having something taken away if one doesn't do the task correctly or well enough will never inspire good riding, but only a resentful, worried, frightened, miserable, athletically rigid kid.

- Take the time to listen intently to what your student is telling you. And, in turn, communicate openly and honestly to the student. If you have a concern, or are upset with a student, privately discuss your thoughts or feelings in a matter-of-fact way, without hysteria, blame, or disapproval. You can get a point across, facilitate change, and be supportive all at the same time.

- Acknowledge out loud how your student is trying to improve or make changes. Let her know that you notice. And don't be stingy with compliments; they are powerful motivators, more so than is criticism.

- Assume benevolence on the part of your student (see The Benevolent Rider in Chapter 10, "The Psychology of Teaching Sport"). Work a riding problem or slump from the same side of the fence as your student by assuming that he *is* listening, *is* trying, *does* want to "get it." Learning to ride rarely fits into a "mind over matter" approach; trust that your student is doing the best he can with whatever psychological and physical resources are available *at that moment,* and find a way to help him mobilize his knowledge and ability—not by yelling, doing more of the (futile) same, or giving up on him.

- Make yourself a model of the courtesy, responsibility, and self-esteem you'd like to see in your riders. That means more, and influences more, than pouting about the poor judging at the horse show.

What to Do If You Suspect Burnout in a Child

If you wonder whether your child or your student may be suffering from burnout, or may be on the brink of it, talk to him or her. Ask the child directly if he or she has been feeling overwhelmed or overly stressed by riding, by the training, or by showing. Would he like to modify some part of the program (show less? trail ride more? have fewer horses to work?)? Is he having as much fun as before? Are there other, non-riding activities he'd like to become involved in? Encourage the child to be candid, and be on the lookout for ways in which you, as a parent or trainer, may have unwittingly elicited the "wrong" answer to these questions (by facial expression, body language, leading remarks).

I remember a very caring riding family that came for consultation because tension was growing between mother and daughter about the balance of riding and other extracurricular activities in the daughter's life. It turned out that the daughter, who had a pretty heavy riding and training schedule, felt she was missing out on some things, especially school-related social events. Specifically, she wanted to try out for the school's softball team. However, she felt that whenever she mentioned this, her mom would get angry and remark how much she and the father had invested in her riding. The mother would then, according to the daughter, say, "Fine! We'll just sell the horses. Go play baseball."

Now, the kid didn't want to give up riding by any stretch of the imagination. She just wanted an afternoon or two a week to hang out with her school buddies and play ball—just to see if she liked it. So far, for years, all her afternoons (and weekends) had been taken up with riding.

This was a case of "the burnout that could have been." A single joint consultation allowed the girl to explain to her parents that she didn't want to quit riding, but that her mother's comments made it hard for her to be honest about how she was feeling. Mom was then able to recognize her overinvestment in the daughter's life and allow the girl the space and independence she needed to make some important decisions on her own. As a result, the daughter was free to love her first and primary sport of riding again, as it no longer kept her from exploring other social and recreational opportunities.

I certainly understand how parents and trainers may react strongly, and negatively, to a talented rider's wanting to "do something else a little bit" when so much time and money have been poured into training, and perhaps into buying good horseflesh. But this is not the child's problem. This is a risk that must be understood from the get-go by the youngster's family and trainer. No child should have to account for wanting more than riding in his or her life or for having a change of heart. And if lines of communication have been open all along then there should be few surprises. I'm not referring to the spoiled or ungrateful child who has casually asked for, and then accepted, lots of extras in terms of family resources, and then one day announces that he is "bored" and done with the whole business. Search here for a more serious problem, such as masked or hidden burnout, a loss of esteem due to not being competitive anymore, an inability or unwillingness to face one's limitations and work to eliminate them, or perhaps even depression. Responsibility, accountability, and active decision-making and feedback on the part of the young rider should be woven into the riding experience, along with the parents' involvement, including those experiences having to do with the degree and frequency of training, the number of horses the child is responsible for, the amount of time devoted to riding, and so on. That approach prevents situations where the youngster "suddenly" bails out of the sport and the parents are left with three unridden horses or ponies on full show board.

Parents and trainers should also be in regular contact about how much is enough and how much is too much. Don't make the mistake of assuming that the "other party" is monitoring the situation. Even the best-intentioned parents and trainers can lose sight of the forest for the trees from time to time, or sometimes parents and trainers may have different tolerances for how much stress is an acceptable part of the sport at competitive levels. Trust each other to have some good insights about the situation that the other doesn't have; each of you sees the child from a different perspective and in a different context (home versus barn), so pooling your data works to everyone's advantage.

What Things Look Like When They're Good Again

- The child seems happy and enthusiastic about riding. There is no "attitude problem."
- The child seems less prone to injury in and around the barn and on horseback.
- Relations between child and parents, child and peers, and child and trainer seem better, less conflicted, lighter, more fun and upbeat.
- The child is eager to improve or to be challenged.
- The child seems to have developed more psychological coping resources, such as time management skills, an ability to relax in the sport setting, the capacity to build and maintain over time a positive social support system, and an ability to feel good about his or her accomplishments apart from whatever praise he or she may be getting from trainers or parents.

Questions from Parents and Trainers

How can I teach the young riders in my barn better sportsmanship? They all give lip service to it, but it seems superficial when I watch their reactions to winning and losing.

There are certain human qualities that are better inspired than taught, and I think that sportsmanship is one of them. The key here is making the dignified and admirable response of good sportsmanship attractive to people, specifically, to young people. I've found that modeling that kind of behavior, and resurrecting the old-fashioned idea of heroes, in the forms of mythical characters and film or public figures, goes much further in promoting sportsmanship and integrity than any lecture will ever do. When I need inspiration for acts of integrity and moral courage, I think of Atticus Finch, from Harper Lee's classic novel *To Kill a Mockingbird*. An attorney in the South during the 1940s, Atticus fights alone to protect the rights of a black man wrongly accused of rape. It is a rich and moving story. Just thinking of Atticus Finch and imagining what he would have done has often put resolve into decisions I've had to make in real life.

Talk with your young riders about the people or fictional characters they like and admire. Do any of the traits identified have relevance for riding? If so, point it out. Discuss with them, too, current and legendary figures in the equestrian world and how they were (or weren't) "horsemen" in the true and noble spirit of the word. Have some of these kids join you in the schooling area or on the rail of a larger show to watch the better-behaved professionals ride and school, win or lose. Observe together how they handle upsets and triumphs and how they treat their colleagues, treat their horses. Make sportsmanship an integral part of the training program at the barn, and it will feel—and be treated—less like an isolated, crusty old topic to be addressed only on special occasions. And, of course, it goes without saying that modeling the desired behavior and attitude goes the furthest of all teaching principles in influencing young people.

My son has been starting to show some pretty ugly sportsmanship at horse shows recently. I don't want to prohibit him from going to horse shows, but his behavior is becoming increasingly out of line. He yanks his pony up after a bad jumping round, ignores his trainer after coming out of the ring, and is plain sour. How should I handle this?

Firmly. First, find out from your son's trainer what he or she has done already to try to correct such behavior. I'd suggest that both you and your trainer then sit down with your son and explain that certain actions will not be tolerated in the future, and they include both those which are unsportsmanlike and inhumane to his pony and those which are disrespectful and unpleasant toward his trainer or parents. Then I'd explain to him that if he's not ready to understand this and behave appropriately, he's not ready to show. Stick to your guns. Showing is a privilege, not an entitlement.

I'm worried that I've become more personally invested in my daughter's riding than is reasonable or healthy. How can I tell if this is true?

You're already a step ahead of the game by being thoughtful enough to have asked this question. If more parents took that first step, there'd probably be a lot fewer unhappy riders out there. I'll refer you to Chapter 14, entitled "The Many Faces of Competition Stress," which highlights symptoms of stress in individuals and in families that show horses, and to the list below of questions to ask yourself to determine whether your personal investment in your daughter's riding is excessive.

- Do I regularly feel angry or disappointed when my daughter does not win or do as well as expected?

- Have I been taking her wins and losses personally, as if they reflect on my mothering, athletic ability, or choices regarding her riding participation?

- Do my daughter and I have more arguments regarding her riding? Do we feel more like adversaries than teammates?

- Do I urge her to go to more shows, lessons, and clinics than she's interested in going to?

- Do my spouse and I agree on the question of our daughter's involvement in riding and on *my* involvement in her riding?

- Do I find myself fantasizing about my daughter's riding professionally or at international levels of competition?

- Do I enjoy bragging about my daughter's accomplishments? Do I embarrass my daughter by what I say to others?

We've come to the end of this chapter on parent and trainer facilitation of sportsmanship in riding and move toward the last, one that speaks to the variety of ways in which serous involvement in equestrian competitive sport can emotionally affect a rider and that rider's family. Since any one person's goals, dreams, success, struggles, and failures both touch and tax the heart and minds of the people with whom they live and interact, it makes sense to talk about how this happens, what it looks like when it does happen, and what to do about it when what has happened doesn't feel very good to those affected.

Chapter Fourteen

The Many Faces
of Competition Stress

WE DON'T LIVE or work in isolation, nor do we ride that way. Our actions and experiences in school or at home or at the office affect not only ourselves but the people with whom we share our lives— family and relatives, friends, roommates, brothers and sisters. It's no different with riding, and while I've covered in earlier chapters how one's personal life can affect one's riding, I've yet to talk about how what happens at the barn, and especially a competitive show barn, can significantly touch those with whom we spend our days. That's what this final chapter is about.

For years now, even though the one in the show ring or arena hasn't been the only person affected by the stress of training and showing, he or she is often the only one considered in any discussion about the stresses of competitive equestrian sports. But what can we say about the impact of an active schedule of training and competing on the family members of the rider? And what about stresses that have nothing to do with show nerves and everything to do with the heavy-duty time and money demands of this sport? What happens when parents or spouses become too worried about their loved ones becoming injured? And aren't there real risks of a nonhorsey husband or daughter feeling left out of all the weekend action? Furthermore, what happens when, during times of exceptional stress, the anxieties of the competitor or rider start manifesting themselves as increasing moodiness or even unrealistic demands? And then of course you begin to wonder how this all effects the trainer, and how a trainer decides when and how it may be appropriate to get involved in the family's handling of these different issues. So you see, competition stress isn't so simple after all.

Stress and the Rider

Riding and showing horses for recreation, sport, business, or pleasure is no stroll in the park. Most people involved in other hobbies are done with their activities in the time it takes us just to assemble our tack. Besides the time demands of riding, and apart from the pressure of competition, there are other complexities and stressors, such as the financial outlay, worries about injury or recurring injury to ourselves, worries about soundness, and maintaining proper care of our horses, among others. But we stay with it because we love it or are good at it or are making a living at it or wouldn't dream of being without horses in our lives. So we're really left only with balance and perspective to help us make the decisions that can keep us, and those closely involved in our lives, enjoying for the long haul what this sport has to offer us. How many examples have you come across of riders or families three or four horses deep into the sport who suddenly and alarmingly realize that no one's enjoying it anymore? That's pretty scary. The key to dealing with stress is catching it before things get that extreme.

How Stress Shows Up for Individuals

Not everything about our psychology is obvious and this is certainly true of the ways in which we show our stress. Take a look at the list below to see if any of these signs have become a too-frequent part of your experience.

- generalized anxiety surrounding lesson or show time;
- chronic or preshow jitters, nervous stomach, insomnia;
- feeling overwhelmed by the responsibilities and time demands of preparing for competition or of competing;
- experiencing doubts about whether or not "it's worth it";
- not looking forward as much to lessons, rides, or shows;
- finding excuses to avoid them;
- chronic irritability, fatigue, or "blues";

- unrealistic fears of injury to you or to your horses;

- increasing frustration with losses at shows;

- horse grooming slipping, or increasing impatience with your animals and their needs;

- guilt over the toll your sport or vocation is taking on the family or household;

- feeling a need to "do well" or win in order to justify keeping or showing the horse.

Now don't count up how many of these you've felt and start looking for some kind of check list to see whether you're a "low," "medium," or "high" scorer. *Any* serious rider is going to find a few things on this list that relate to himself or herself. Like any competitive enterprise, horse showing is stressful, and periods of ambivalence and burnout come with the territory. A better question to ask yourself than how many of these things you have ever experienced is the following: *Am I experiencing enough of these things for a long enough period of time that it has begun to worry me or those around me?* Another good one is: *Am I still enjoying this?*

With more people keeping their animals at home, or doing more of their own grooming and horse management at the barn, the risks of being stretched too thin and feeling overwhelmed are pretty high. But this is almost always a manageable problem, because there are things you can do to change your situation. Feeling overwhelmed becomes an issue only when you feel there's nothing you can do to change anything. Many riders who I know get stuck *there;* they are so busy getting the barn work done or getting the kids off to school before running out the door for a lesson that they can't even begin to consider how any of it could be different. *"Who has time even to stop and think these days?"* they say. And, *"Even if I did stop to think, I wouldn't know what to think about that could make a difference. What I need is more time / a better horse / classier tack / a more understanding wife / husband / trainer / mother / father!"*

Well, there *are* things you can do to reduce the stress in your life that's related to your riding. These things don't involve a miracle and they don't involve a lot of time either. Reducing stress often can be boiled down to doing something different. One little thing may be enough to set the ball rolling; *this* is the key. You get started on a new plan, a new idea, a new perspective, a new outlook, a new approach, and go from there. Unfreeze the status quo. Always consider what could be. And, most important, keep things moving and changing if they're not working. Don't do more of the same; better a wrong choice than none at all.

Bear this in mind, too: many people don't ever start anything new or look to see how things might be different because they think that changes have to be BIG IMPORTANT ones. Any good navigator knows that you need to change only one or two degrees on your compass point to move off in a whole new direction.

What You Can Do to Eliminate, Reduce, and Deal with Stress

- Something, anything, just do something different! Don't fall into the trap of believing that there is nothing you can do about the stressors you experience. Nip in the bud any sense of helplessness or hopelessness about making things better. You simply aren't that unresourceful, or you wouldn't have picked such a demanding sport to begin with.

- Make the effort to find the babysitter who will watch your eight-year-old at the barn so that you can really pay attention to what you and your horse are doing rather than to whether or not Mikey is in the manure pit again.

- Pack that Playmate or Igloo with a fresh turkey breast sandwich so that you're not stuck for the third straight day with a sausage grinder and fries.

- Add the extra lesson a week you think will make the difference in being prepared for the Nationals.

- Tell your spouse just how much his or her presence at a show means to you and that you'd really like him or her there this Saturday. Would he or she come, please?

- Commit to getting seven hours of sleep the night before the next show, even if it means that Mom and the kids or Dad and the kids eat out that night and put themselves to bed. You—in bed at nine, and lights out in thirty minutes.

- Prepare *now* for your next show instead of waiting until the last minute. Boots shined on a Wednesday will still be shiny on Saturday. A ratcatcher pressed on Monday will still have its creases on Sunday. Show tack cleaned on Wednesday will be most respectable still on Friday. Show pads washed and bleached on Friday will still look washed and bleached two Fridays later. You get the point.

- If you want your husband, wife, sister, uncle, business partner, or secretary to ask you more about your riding, *tell* him or her! What someone worries would be an imposition often turns out to be a very welcome invitation to become involved.

Dealing with Performance Demands, Real or Imagined

Performance demands are a big source of stress for the competitive rider. They may be real (other people and the rider himself or herself pushing for the winning ride time after time after time) or imagined (a rider falsely perceives others to be pushing for winning rides all the time, when in fact these others are comfortable with different or lesser goals). It doesn't matter which it is: they feel the same.

Sometimes show riders (adults and children) who are uncomfortable with, or unaware of, their self-critical or perfectionist tendencies may experience the demand to do well as coming from *outside* themselves rather than from within. They worry about disappointing a mother, a grandfather, or a husband, or worry that unless they win prizes or money or recognition there will be little justification to continue the sport. Trainers who ride for owners are especially—and understandably—vulnerable to these concerns, as their professional reputations and livelihoods depend on good (often translated to mean *winning*) rides. Real or imagined, expectations and demands to do well can be an enormous source of anxiety that threatens a rider's performance level.

A million times I've heard the lament, *"Why can't I ride as well at shows as I do at home?"* The reason is that the winning ride is not simply a matter of volition; you cannot "will" yourself to ride your best. You can remind yourself to carry your hands, keep your leg on, open your shoulders, or keep your eyes up, but you can't make yourself "ride perfectly." Good riding is certainly thoughtful, but it is also fluid, rhythmic, and instinctive. And none of these qualities is a voluntary response of the human body, that is, a response that can be commanded to appear. Instead, each is a response that will happen when allowed to happen, and that usually means as the natural outgrowth of feeling comfortable with and confident about what you are doing as a rider.

One wonderful answer to dealing with performance demands lies in transcending them, that is, getting "above" them in some manner. Transcending performance demands similarly involves recognizing that talent shows itself in numerous and subtle ways throughout a ride. This is an especially useful perspective for those of you who can feel that it is enough to ride well, without needing to win. Because then for you it becomes possible to rise to the occasion of riding well anytime—at home schooling, in the warm-up area, or even when walking with quiet dignity out of the show ring. The ability to command respect from your fellow riders, family members, or colleagues is then available in many more opportunities than you had thought; it is available in how you speak about your wins and losses, how you treat your animals, how they and you are presented—not just at the shows but around the barn as well—the grace with which you handle a wrong lead, a refusal to jump, a spooky horse, an unsound horse, a bad lesson, a bad show. A winning rider is not always the one with the blue ribbons. For more reading on dealing with performance pressures, refer to Chapter 12, "Work Stress and the Trainer-Instructor."

Stress and the Family

For the past several decades, mental health professionals all over the world have recognized the importance of understanding people not just as individuals but in the context of their environment. The truth is that people always act and react to one another. Some like to say they function in "systems"—loosely organized, interactive feedback loops in which everyone responds to both the spoken and unspoken desires and needs of those with whom they are emotionally connected. A husband and father of four becomes sick and disabled one month after the youngest child has gone off to college. He becomes depressed, his wife angry. Neither of them realizes that he is responding to her fears of not being needed by anyone once the kids flew the coop. A generally well-behaved boy acts up in grade school in an unwitting attempt to gain the attention of his parents, who are too caught up in their work. In these and other real-life examples, what would be considered a "symptom" is also, or even alternately, a communication of sorts, a way of saying (in the first example) *"Don't worry. I'll make sure you'll feel needed around here,"* or (in the second) *"Don't ignore me, please, Mom and Dad."* The communicator often doesn't even realize that he or she is sending a message, and the receiver often doesn't realize it either. People simply respond to each other at multiple levels. This is a hard truth for those of us who like to believe that we are in control of everything we do, captains of our own ships.

How Stress Shows Up for the Family

The following are ways in which a family may show its strain. Experiencing any of these very intensely or very frequently, or experiencing several at a time, is a clue that something needs more attention.

- The family comes home from a show and everyone's irritable with one another or nobody is talking to anyone else;

- The showing member doesn't want any family members coming to the horse shows;

- The non-showing parent or child begins to feel a sense of dread around horse show days;

- A parent starts thinking, "I don't know what to say to her anymore" (about either losing or winning);

- A parent or sibling feels used or inappropriately treated around the barn or at horse shows (i.e., "Dad, go get me a hoof pick. No, not that one! Oh, forget it!");

- Worries mount about time management or money matters;
- There are more squabbles than usual; people snapping at each other;
- It doesn't seem as if anyone's having much of a good time.

Families as Part of the Solution, Not Part of the Problem

Many people, when thinking about riders and their families, consider the family to be a source of the stress rather than a resource for solutions. As a psychologist and therapist who counsels riding families, and sees that what was once a lot of fun is turning into a lot of stress, I find that most families can better overcome the tensions caused by the riding when they do it together, rather than by considering it all the "rider's" problem. They do this best by seeing themselves as a team, and dealing with problems and stressors from the same side of the fence, instead of focusing on their frustration with the person or people thought to be "causing" the problem. Pooling emotional resources, listening to one another's perspectives, and working collectively on solutions are the name of the game in such family consultations. A quick sampling of these problems and stressors of equestrian competitive sport may include: perceived pressures to win; resentments; jealousies; guilt; safety fears; worries about money. Many times the problems are not obvious and show up in a child's not wanting to go to as many shows, or in a parent's making some angry or sarcastic remark. Other times a problem is obvious, but no one in the family feels he or she can say anything about it. On yet other occasions, people just don't know what to do, so they simply hope that the uncomfortable feeling or the riding slump will resolve itself.

Some More on Family Matters

Kids are very perceptive of and loyal to their parents' anxieties and will often act these out in their riding. I know of one ten-year-old boy who enacted his father's (covert) resentment about all the money that was being poured into the riding. He did this by developing a fear of jumping and a desire to change sports. Neither the child nor the parents recognized the boy's change of heart as a response to the father's nonverbal communication (people have tons of ways to communicate their displeasure without using words), and, in fact, the father himself wasn't aware that he was sending out such a message. Once Mom and Dad did become aware, however, they and their son were able to discuss the money worries and set reasonable spending limits, which alleviated both the father's anxiety and the boy's guilt. The riding continued, and the boy's fear of jumping subsided.

Family members sometimes unknowingly project their own fears onto one another to the point where it can be hard for them to determine realistically what's safe to do on horseback and what's not. A father wrestling with his own lack of bravado and courage may inadvertently encourage his child or spouse to take riding risks in order to shore up his own sense of courage. Owning up to our anxieties and insecurities keeps us from drawing others into these troubles.

Difficulty in understanding another's perspective can cause tensions, too. A rider's sibling, brave and aggressive on the football field, may not be sympathetic to his brother's fears about getting run away with on horseback, and may make him feel ashamed. Talking together as a family about what is and what isn't supportive for the rider is often a relief not only to the rider but to everyone else who has tried to help, only to find that his or her attempts have just made things worse.

A parent who stands at the rail of each horse show tabulating the points needed for championship is sure to ruin everybody's (rider's, trainer's, other family members') enjoyment of a show. One family I met with in which this was happening, and which had three riding children, became able to joke with Dad about his "scoreboard," and set up rules for when he could calculate points. I also had the kids make a deal with Dad: each time they caught him tabulating points, they were able to get out *their* "scorecards" and rate him on his parenting duties! The family began once again to enjoy showing, and most important, began again to enjoy each other.

Things for Families to Try at Home

- Try being more observant. Learn to become aware of, and sensitive to, changes in the family's mood and interactions. You don't need (or want) to become a sleuth, but oblivion is any family's worst enemy. If you're not sure about how the kids feel about the upcoming horse show, ask them. Ask your spouse. Ask yourself. Keep your eyes *and* mouth open.

- Talk more. Tell more. Discuss your thoughts regarding all this showing and training and getting up early and so on. Talking about it isn't the same as complaining or whining; it means simply inviting everyone's private (and likely very similar) thoughts out for a verbal romp. Try not to slip into these all-too-human and all-too-common inhibiting thought patterns:

  — If I pretend not to notice that anything's different around here, I won't have to do or say anything about it . . .

  — Since I have no idea how to bring up these observations or thoughts or worries, I won't . . .

  — Everyone will think I'm imagining things . . .

  — Everyone will say I worry or think too much . . .

  — Everyone will tell me to stop analyzing everything . . .

  — Everyone will get into a fight . . .

  However, if you do slip into one, here's what you can say to your family to help get you started:

  — "This may seem to come out of left field, but is anyone else around here feeling really stressed out by the last month of showing?"

  — "Sometimes, kids, I worry that Mom and I are the only ones still having fun with the horses. Is it possible?"

  — "How can we help you feel more comfortable and less nervous at shows?"

  — "How can I be more helpful around the barn? I've been feeling a little left out of the swing of things."

  — "I'm game to help out, kiddo, but manners at the barn are as important as they are at home."

- Hold a low-key family bull session to mull over how people are enjoying (or not) their summer, new horses, new trainer, and so on.

- Consider a family consultation or family-and-trainer consultation with a sport psychologist to troubleshoot and come up with workable, appealing solutions.

Protect Your Love of the Sport

You know, you didn't get into riding because you were looking for more stress in your life. If you're not enjoying what you're doing, that's your cue to make a change. Don't wait for it to get better; *do* something to make it better. It's so important that you do whatever you can to preserve the sentiment that drew you into riding in the first place.

And so we've come to the end. This last chapter was written to expand the principles of sport and family psychology to a larger community than just the rider and trainer so that family and others closely involved with the rider can better enjoy the rider's experiences with horses. This book was never intended to be just for riders; it was designed as a resource for all those involved directly or indirectly with riders. I hope there's something in it for everyone, and that everyone takes the liberty to let his or her buffet plate look a little different from the plates of others. Digest what you have, and come back for more. Chef's gone home, but this smorgasbord stays open all day, all night.

Notes

FRONT MATTER

p. ix   Quote from Alan Watts and quote from Henry Ford: Both quotes cited from *Thinking Body, Doing Mind: Tao Sports for Extraordinary Performance in Athletics, Business and Life,* Huang & Lynch, (1992).

CHAPTER ONE: THE MAGIC IN SPORTS PSYCHOLOGY

p. 11   Wylie quote: *People* magazine, March 2, 1992.

CHAPTER TWO: BREAKING MYTHS ABOUT RELAXATION

p. 18   Unestähl study: Unestahl, L., Hypnotic preparation of athletes, in G. Burrows, D. Collison, and L. Dennerstein (eds.), *Hypnosis,* North Holland: Elsevier (1979).

p. 19   Andre Agassi quote: *Sports Illustrated Presents Future Legends: The 20 Brightest Young Stars in Sports* (1995).

p. 29   Taoist teachings: *Thinking Body, Doing Mind: Tao Sports for Extraordinary Performance in Athletics, Business and Life,* Huang & Lynch (1992).

CHAPTER THREE: IDEOMOTOR TRAINING

p. 34   Sustaining mental concentration for tournaments: Margeneau, E., *Sports Without Pressure,* New York: Gardner Press (1990).

CHAPTER FOUR: MENTAL REHEARSAL: NEW TWISTS ON AN OLD STORY

p. 45   Thorpe dominating the Olympic Games: Carey, A., *The Philadelphia Enquirer* (1994).

p. 46   Two sports psychologists: Feltz, D. L., and Landers, D. M., The effects of mental practice on motor skill learning and performance: A meta-analysis, *Journal of Sport Psychology,* 5, 25–57 (1983).

p. 50   Nancy Ditz quote: Ungerleider, S., and Golding, J. M., *Beyond strength: Psychological profiles of Olympic athletes,* Iowa: Wm. C. Brown (1992).

p. 58   Soviet team preparing for 1976 summer Olympics: Vealey,

R. S. Imagery training for performance enhancement. In J. M. Williams (ed.), *Applied sport psychology: Personal growth for peak performance,* Palo Alto: Mayfield Press (1986).

p. 59   Using imagery in preparation and training: Nideffer, R. M., *Athlete's guide to mental training,* Illinois: Human Kinetics Publishing (1985).

CHAPTER FIVE: HYPNOSIS AND SELF-HYPNOSIS

p. 65   Allusion to hypnotic phenomena: Edgette and Edgette, *The Handbook of Hypnotic Phenomena in Psychotherapy.* New York: Brunner-Mazel (1995).

CHAPTER TEN: THE PSYCHOLOGY OF TEACHING SPORT

p. 145   Child's self-perception: Weiss, M. R., Children in sport: An educational model. In Murray, S. M. (ed.), *Sport Psychology Interventions.* Illinois: Human Kinetics (1995).

p. 145   "desire for excellence": Crabtree, H., *Saddle Seat Equitation.* New York: Doubleday Equestrian Library (1970).

CHAPTER THIRTEEN: TO THE PARENTS AND TRAINERS OF YOUNG RIDERS

p. 194   Eric Margenau: Margenau, E., *Sports Without Pressure: A Guide for Parents and Coaches of Young Athletes,* New York: Brunner-Mazel (1990).

p. 194   Athletes' Valuable Life Skills: Danish, S. J., Petitpas, A., and Hale, B. D., Psychology interventions: A life development model, in S. Murphy (ed.), *Sport Psychology Interventions,* Illinois: Human Kinetics (1995).

p. 195   Weiss chapter: Weiss, M. R., in S. Murphy (ed.), op. cit.

p. 196   Effects of overtraining: McCann, S., Overtraining and burnout, in S. Murphy (ed.), op. cit.

p. 198   Tips on preventing burnout: Adapted from "How to Be a Winning Parent: A Parent (and Coach's) Guide for Winning in the Youth Sports Game," a handout prepared by Dr. Alan Goldberg, *Competitive Advantage,* Amherst, MA.

p. 200   Tips that can help a kid enjoy riding: adapted from "A Coaches Guide to Developing Self-Esteem," a handout prepared by Dr. Alan Goldberg, op. cit.

About the Author

DR. JANET SASSON EDGETTE is a clinical and sports psychologist practicing in the western suburbs of Philadelphia. She is also a founding codirector of the Brief Therapy Center of Philadelphia and codirector of the Milton H. Erickson Institute of Philadelphia, a private facility offering general counseling services to individuals, couples, and families, as well as training programs on hypnosis and psychotherapy to area mental health professionals. Janet is a frequently invited speaker and workshop leader in both the mental health and equestrian industries, traveling around the nation and internationally as well. Some of the well-recognized meetings at which she has taught include four international Congresses on Ericksonian Approaches to Hypnosis and Psychotherapy (Los Angeles, Phoenix) and two Eastern (U.S.) Conferences on Ericksonian Hypnosis and Psychotherapy (Philadelphia); the Family Therapy Networker Conference (Washington, D.C.), the American Horse Shows Association

Convention, the American Saddlebred Horse Association Convention, the American Hunter-Jumper Foundation Young Rider Seminars, and the Women and Horses Conference; and conferences of the Pennsylvania Psychological Association, the United Professional Horseman's Association, and the American Riding Instructor's Certification Program, among others. She has been featured in a variety of magazines and publications, including *Practical Horseman, Hoof Print, Hunter & Sport Horse, American Horse Shows Association Horse Show, Horse & Rider,* and *The Morgan Horse.*

Janet has also authored a dozen professional articles and book chapters on various aspects of her work as a clinical and sports psychologist, and now writes a monthly column for *Practical Horseman* magazine. In addition to *Heads Up!,* Janet has coauthored a psychotherapy text entitled *The Handbook of Hypnotic Phenomena in Psychotherapy.* Janet also has hosted a monthly radio show on sports psychology, *Horse Sense* (WCOJ-AM, Coatesville, Pa.), where listeners called in with questions.

A large portion of Janet's practice involves sports performance enhancement and counseling for riders, and sometimes their families, of all different equestrian disciplines—hunter, jumper, dressage, eventing, fox hunting, trail, endurance, western, saddle seat, fine harness, and driving. Such work includes, but is not limited to, mental preparation for shows and events, general anxiety reduction, overcoming fears or bad riding habits, building or rebuilding confidence, modifying one's self-image as a rider or an athlete, helping trainers prepare students (or sometimes parents or spouses) for the mental demands of training and competing, and helping families deal constructively with the pressures and the time and financial demands of the sport. Janet works with both competitive and recreational riders, offering private sessions and group clinics on and off her office site. Besides the larger industry meetings mentioned above, she also speaks to local riding associations and clubs, and frequently to collections of young riders. Janet also works with professionals in the equestrian industry, offering consultations on performance, training, business, and client/customer-related issues.

Janet herself has been a rider for over thirty years, having competed in the equitation, hunter, and jumper divisions around the eastern part of the United States as a teenager, qualifying for all the major year-end national finals. She made the call-backs for both the AHSA Medal and ASPCA Maclay classes held in Harrisburg and New York, respectively, in the early 1970s. She currently rides and competes regularly in the jumper divisions of regional horse shows.